ANCIENT ART

AT THE ART INSTITUTE OF CHICAGO

The
Art Institute
of
Chicago

MUSEUM STUDIES

VOLUME 20, NO. 1

The Art Institute of Chicago
MUSEUM STUDIES

VOLUME 20, NO. 1

Ancient Art at The Art Institute of Chicago

Foreword

To a layman who has never seen its collections, mention of The Art Institute of Chicago most often, I think, conjures an image of paintings, and in particular of Impressionist and Post-Impressionist paintings. This is not unreasonable, since one of the greatest glories of the Institute does surely lie in that field; but it was certainly not the intention of the founders to create simply a picture-gallery, let alone a gallery devoted primarily to the modern painting (as Impressionism and Post-Impressionism then were) of the western world. The Art Institute began as a practical school of painting and sculpture, and it was not at once that the idea was developed of backing the art school with a collection of works of older art. That, though, did come soon; and from those beginnings the Art Institute became what it is today: a magnificent museum illustrating the history of art in a wide sweep; and, attached but separate, a school of creative art.

As rich and as splendidly presented as the wide-ranging picture galleries are the collections of material from the Far East; and one could point to many other outstanding displays. The field, however, to which this volume is devoted, the arts of the ancient Mediterranean, has been for some time in no position to make such an impression, owing to extreme constriction of gallery space; a situation the rectification of which is here celebrated. At the period of the Art Institute's foundation there was no doubt, in the minds of most people who took an interest in art, that the true art tradition was that of Renaissance and post-Renaissance Europe, and that the foundation of that great classical tradition was laid in Greece and Rome. As Karen Alexander mentions in the opening essay, the new Art Institute inherited from its predecessor, the Chicago Academy of Fine Arts, a large collection of plaster casts of Greek and Roman sculpture, from which the students drew. When, a little later, the imaginative expansion of the art school by the creation of a collection of original works from the past began to take shape, the arts of Rome, Etruria, and Greece, and those of the great centers, from which the Greeks themselves first took inspiration, in the Near East and especially Egypt, were all early represented by purchase and generous gift.

The interest in these fields continued over the years; and as will be seen from the essays and pictures in this special issue of *Museum Studies*, as well as in the new permanent collection galleries themselves, this is a representative and often impressive collection. That it does not quite rival the greatest of the museum's holdings is due perhaps, at least in part, to the fact that ancient art, though money was early earmarked for the specific purpose of purchasing classical antiquities, has never had an independent department with its own curator. Those responsible, the curators of the departments within which this material was housed as well as the assistants and associates directly concerned with looking after it, have done heroic work in organizing acquisitions (often through the great generosity of citizens of Chicago), conservation, and displays; but there has been nobody who had the authority to push its claims exclusively and strongly against other interests.

I spoke of the special place the arts of Greece and Rome held in Western thought in the period when the Art Institute was founded. Today we look beyond the Western tradition, and have a far wider appreciation of the range of character great art can take. By a natural reaction against its former tyranny, the classical tradition is now sometimes denigrated or dismissed, but that surely is a profound mistake. The Greeks laid the foundations of one of the great traditions of world art. They took their own start from the art of Egypt and the Near East; their achievements were channeled to Europe through the art of imperial Rome; and these three great linked traditions retain a position of fundamental importance in the history of world art. That these facts are appreciated in Chicago is shown no less by the new display galleries and the essays in this admirable volume than by the success of the Classical Art Society. That imaginative venture, of relatively recent creation, has evoked warm and generous response in the city. We may surely now look forward to a flourishing period in the history of Mediterranean antiquities in the Art Institute.

MARTIN ROBERTSON
Cambridge, England

Acknowledgments

This special issue of *Museum Studies* can be directly attributed to the inspiration and dedication of the Classical Art Society. Wishing to support the reinstallation of ancient art at The Art Institute of Chicago, the Society proposed a publication that would provide scholarly discussion of a number of objects in the collection and would reach a wide audience. Classical Art Society President Elizabeth Gebhard, acting at the suggestion of Kim Coventry and Ann Cole, recommended this project to the Society. This proposal was enthusiastically accepted, and the Society's Board, led by Louise Holland, Jackie Haffenberg, Joan Wagner, and Bonnie Pritchard, committed itself to raising funds to realize this goal. The Classical Art Society could not have chosen a better way to extend the utility of the new Galleries of Ancient Art than by promoting this succinctly written and attractively illustrated introduction to the collection.

We are grateful to the scholars for their contributions to this issue. Senior Staff Photographer Bob Hashimoto took new photographs of most of the objects especially for this publication. Karen Alexander's useful history of the collection is but one of her many services to this enterprise. Research Assistant Mary Greuel shouldered most of the burden of this issue's organization. Ann Wassmann, Associate Director of the Department of Graphic Design and Communication Services, designed the book's graceful layout. Finally, editor Michael Sittenfeld, supported by Robert Sharp, Manine Golden, and others in the Publications Department, shaped this volume with his accustomed care.

Ian Wardropper
Eloise W. Martin Curator of European Decorative Arts and Sculpture, and Classical Art

---

Each entry in this issue is followed by its author's initials. The authors and their initials are:

ET	Emily Teeter
TGD	Theresa Gross-Diaz
JGP	John Griffiths Pedley
RD	Richard De Puma
CCV	Cornelius C. Vermeule III
KTL	Kurt T. Luckner

Entries on ancient coins, which appear in the sections on Egyptian, Greek, and Roman art, are by Theresa Gross-Diaz, Assistant Professor of History at Loyola University of Chicago.

Artworks in this issue are referred to by catalogue number (cat. no.).

In addition to those individuals mentioned in the acknowledgments, the editor would also like to thank the following Art Institute staff members who contributed to this issue: Katherine Houck Fredrickson, Cris Ligenza, Adam Jolles, Kathleen Hartman, Pam Stuedemann, Christopher K. Gallagher, Chester Brummel, and Sally Bernard.

A History of the Ancient Art Collection at The Art Institute of Chicago

KAREN ALEXANDER

The Art Institute of Chicago

The ancient art collection of The Art Institute of Chicago may have been founded in plaster, but, like Caesar's Rome, it has been rebuilt in marble, as well as bronze, limestone, glass, and gold. The Art Institute's progenitor, the Chicago Academy of Fine Arts, taught its students painting and sculpture. Its collection consisted of scores of plaster casts of Greek and Roman sculpture from which hopeful students could practice "drawing from the antique." From 1879, when the Academy was founded, to 1889, when the Art Institute made its first purchases of original ancient art, the founders' energies were consumed by establishing and maintaining the physical buildings, offering classes, and mounting exhibitions. By 1889, driven by the expansive vision of its thirty-five-year-old president, Charles L. Hutchinson, and its director, William M. R. French, the museum's board of trustees envisioned a permanent collection. To the nineteenth-century mind, nothing was more permanent or primal than the art of Egypt, Greece, and Rome.

Interest in the ancient past had been stimulated by the discovery of the ruins of Pompeii in 1748 and the unearthing of Egypt's monuments following Napoleon's Egyptian campaign in 1798. Not only scholars, but writers, architects, and furnituremakers wallowed in the excitement of recently discovered cultural artifacts from the period of the Old and New Testaments. Egypt, buried under sand, and Pompeii, obscured in A.D. 79 under the ash of Mount Vesuvius, became the impetus for renewed study of the past in a physically provable context. Napoleon's court furnishings, the English Adams brothers' Pompeian fireplace mantels, women's hairdos à la Sappho, and sphinxes on teacups attest to Neoclassicism's enormous popularity. America, which envisioned its government as a fusion of Greek democracy and Roman republicanism, applied Neoclassicism to its culture for its philosophical as well as its aesthetic value. In the nineteenth century, this took the form of Federal-style furniture, Jupiter's eagle on coinage, and bank buildings with Doric columns. Museums reacted to the public's interest by buying or excavating antiquities to fill their galleries.

Symbols of permanence and eternal verity were important to Chicago's civic leaders, who had watched their fledgling city go up in flames in 1871. Many of Chicago's cultural leaders had come from cities on the Eastern seaboard where museums were a necessary component of culture, and those with aspirations to have comprehensive collections began their displays with the contents of Egyptian tombs and with shelves of painted Greek pots. Following the lead of the eighteenth-century German archaeologist Johann Joachim Winckelmann, collectors as well as scholars, and interested amateurs, believed that the arts of the Mediterranean world constituted the exemplar from which all subsequent Western art evolved. In a speech to the Chicago Literary Club, Hutchinson echoed the academic nineteenth-century view that the "true mission of art is to discover and represent the ideal."[1] The duty of the cultural leader was to offer the public beautiful objects that would lift and purify the viewers' spirit and behavior. It was inevitable

FIGURE 1. Gallery with plaster casts of Egyptian and Assyrian sculpture at The Art Institute of Chicago, 1917.

FIGURE 2. During their trip to Europe in 1889, William M. R. French (1843–1914), first director of the Art Institute, and Charles L. Hutchinson (1854–1924), president of the museum's board of trustees, purchased classical works for the Art Institute's collection. French took notes and made drawings in a small notebook as they traveled, often jotting his observations on European museums. On this page from his notebook, French sketched ancient Greek vases that he and Hutchinson bought for the Art Institute; the vase at the top is a hydria (water jar) (cat. no. 21), and the second vase from the top is the name vase of the Chicago Painter (cat. no. 27).

FIGURE 3. Another page from French's travel notebook.

that ancient art, whose associations with both Aristotle and the Bible guaranteed an intellectual imprimatur, should be the collection of choice.

From early record ledgers, it appears that the museum's first purchase of original antiquities was a group of 150 terracotta statuettes (see, for example, cat. no. 30) and fragments acquired from Francis H. Bacon of Boston.[2] Bacon was an amateur archaeologist who had accompanied a friend to the coast of Turkey to identify a likely excavation site for the newly founded Archaeological Institute of America. When Assos was chosen as the site, Bacon stayed on as assistant to the director of the excavation.[3] On private sorties through the countryside, Bacon gathered fragments of terracotta statuettes made in the fourth and third centuries B.C. The collection that the Art Institute later purchased from him is identified as coming from Smyrna and environs, and while the group itself is absolutely authentic, it contains few outstanding pieces. Its meagerness represents, in a touching way, the museum's first tentative steps into world-class collecting.

The museum's next venture into collecting was more ambitious. After being authorized by George Armour, treasurer of the board of trustees, to spend $1,000 on "objects,"[4] Hutchinson and French set off on a European buying trip. Although they overspent their budget by $154, Hutchinson and French were able to gather together a rich assortment of Greek vases (see, for example, cat. nos. 20 and 27; see also figs. 2–3), Roman sculpture, and two portions of Roman lead water pipe,

for which Mr. French spent $1.94 of his own money.[5] Their advisers ranged from the Roman archaeologist Rodolpho Lanciani to Pio Marinangeli and Augusto Alberici, antiquities dealers in Rome.[6]

Lanciani was both an archaeologist and a historian of the archaeology of the Italian peninsula. An advisor to the Museum of Fine Arts in Boston, he was accustomed to dealing with Americans, and he had even visited Boston in 1888.[7] He conducted his archaeological work with his own team of workers, whom he described as belonging "to a tribe of hereditary excavators. The best cannot read or write. They have an instinct about excavating."[8] Lanciani could be trusted not only to guide the novice purchaser's selection, but also to facilitate the restoration of vases, the cleaning of marbles, and the shipping of crates to the Middle West.

Because the Greek vases that Hutchinson and French bought in Italy had presumably been unearthed from Etruscan tombs, they entered the museum as "Etruscan," and although one vase carried the dealer's assurance that it was "stuck together, no pieces added," some vases were not all they should have been. After they were cleaned in the 1920s, a few were found to be pastiches composed of disparate parts, plaster, and paint, and were probably the work of a certain Francesco Raimondo of Capua.[9] The majority of the vases in this first purchase, however, still constitute the proud anchor of the collection. Forty of the vases were bought from the collection of Augusto Mele, a judge and Neapolitan collector.[10] There seem to have been a number of middlemen such as the Reverend J. C. Fletcher who "effected" the negotiations between the museum and the judge.[11] Clergymen appear repeatedly in these early transactions as either collectors or facilitators. Their long residence in foreign countries as missionaries, their classical education, and their unquestioned probity provided them with an indispensable if unlikely role in the antiquities trade.

Among the works in the shipment from Italy was a stamnos (cat. no. 27) by the artist who came to be known as the Chicago Painter (see drawing in fig. 2). This vase is the paradigm used by Sir John Beazley to identify an anonymous painter of wine storage jars in fifth-century B.C. Athens. Other painters represented in the museum's first buying trip are Douris (cat. no. 24) and the Penthesilea Painter. All three of these painters were popular with buyers in ancient Italy, as shown by the number of their vases found in Italian tombs.

How knowledgeable Hutchinson or French were about Greek vases and their production is unknown, but their selection shows clearly that they sought variety in both vase shape and decoration ranging from a sixth-century hydria (cat. no. 21) for storing water to a series of fifth-century B.C. red-figure Attic cups and amphorae to fourth-century vases made in the Greek colonies of southern Italy (see fig. 4). Hutchinson also bought some Greek vases for his private collection that appear in a 1902 portrait of him painted by Gari Melchers (fig. 5). Hutchinson's private holdings came to the Art Institute after his death in 1924 as a gift from his widow.

The Roman sculpture acquired on the first buying trip was less ambitious presumably because of the museum's investment in its collection of casts. No complete statues were acquired, only marble portrait heads, a terracotta head of Silenus, a pair of hands, and a statuette of Hercules that were all bought from the dealer Augusto Alberici, who doubtless supplied their rather romantic provenances: "found in the Forum of Augustus," "found near Colosseum in a brewery," or "found October, 1888 in Hadrian's villa."[12]

The museum's initial foray into the murky waters of international antiquities markets was so successful that the new holdings were immediately installed in a prominent gallery and accompanied by the museum's first catalogue, which clearly differentiates the cast collection from the original works of art.[13]

In 1890, Hutchinson, accompanied by his friend and fellow philanthropist Martin A. Ryerson, visited the sales rooms of the Hôtel Drouot in Paris to bid on antiquities from the collection of Eugene Piot.[14] The largest purchase was of sixteen pieces of ancient glass. A smattering of Greek terracottas and some vases completed this group of acquisitions. While in Paris, Hutchinson and Ryerson also patronized the firm of Rollin and Feuardent, from whom they bought an unfortunate group of nineteenth-century terracotta statuettes purported to be fourth-century B.C. works made in the Greek city of Tanagra, which was famous for its small terracottas. Cloyingly sweet in expression and contorted into dramatic poses, these figurines are interesting examples of nineteenth-century taste and the demands of nineteenth-century collectors upon the antiquities market. Rollin and Feuardent sold many of these terracottas; whether they did it knowingly or were themselves duped is not known, but Alfred Emerson, the Art Institute's first curator of classical antiquities, identified them as "forged, probably by George Gayas of Piraeus (Greece). . .I know him and his work well. . .Rollin and Feuardent have retailed quantities of his stuff to their much advantage."[15]

Emerson's full-time employment was as a professor of Greek at Lake Forest University in Illinois (now

FIGURE 4. Installation of "Graeco-Italian vases" at the Art Institute, 1901. This installation shows that French and Hutchinson selected classical vases for the museum's collection based partly on their variety of shape and decoration. The sixth vase from the left, bottom row, is a pyxis (container for personal objects) featured in this issue (cat. no. 18). Photo: The Art Institute of Chicago, *General Catalogue of Paintings, Sculpture, and Other Objects of Art in the Museum, August, 1901*, n. pag.

known as Lake Forest College). His weekly visits to the Art Institute's collection were devoted to cataloguing and classifying the antiquities and the casts. He organized an exhibit called the "Collection of Idols" from various cultures[16] and he spruced up the shopworn casts. In 1891, he was hired by Cornell University to teach classics. Emerson continued, however, as the curator in absentia at the Art Institute for twenty-five years, returning now and then to initiate an exhibition or oversee the bronzing of some of the casts, to clean Greek vases and act as custodian to the collection. One of his most spectacular projects was the 1892 show entitled "The Polychrome Exhibition," which included a group of plaster casts from Boston, polychromed with tinted wax and gilding.[17] Emerson added three original Roman sculptures from the Art Institute's collection to the exhibition that he colored in pastel; he stated that it would have been "indiscreet to try wax on original antiques."[18] Unlike curators today, he appears never to have involved himself with museum purchases that were guided by the director and trustees.

In the late nineteenth century, Chicago was a small community. The museum's trustees were the prominent civic leaders, but they were also friends who belonged to the same clubs, summered at the same resorts, and sat on the same boards of businesses and charities. One of Hutchinson's roles as museum president was to motivate other trustees and their friends to underwrite the museum's early purchases. At trustee meetings, individuals pledged to pay for objects that had been previously purchased by Hutchinson and Ryerson in their effort to secure objects on the art market. This flexible financing arrangement, however, did not always work smoothly. In 1915, the trustees were badgered by Hutchinson to pay Ryerson the remainder of his loan that brought the museum, among other things, its magnificent mummy case (cat. no. 7).[19] A fund was tapped to offset part of the debt, but even Hutchinson could not move his board, and Ryerson quietly absorbed the loss.

In 1890, the Art Institute recorded its first accession to the Egyptian collection: a rather common shawabty (mummiform statuette) from the Twenty-Sixth Dynasty given by Amelia B. Edwards, the British founder of the Egyptian Exploration Fund. The purpose of the Fund was to excavate sites in Egypt, sharing the discoveries between the Egyptian government and the institutions involved in the Fund. Museums and universities, unable or unwilling to mount their own foreign excavations, could belong to this archaeological mutual fund for the payment of $750 per year. Since Charles Hutchinson had been instrumental in establishing the Chicago branch of the Fund in 1883,[20] this presentation from Miss Edwards could be seen as a votive offering, or as a blandishment for further involvement. For the next twenty years, the Art Institute faded in and out of the Fund, receiving a division of the spoils being excavated by William M. Flinders Petrie, the great pioneer of modern Egyptian archaeology. James H. Breasted, founder of the Oriental Institute of the University of Chicago, urged the museum to support the excavations and thereby build the museum's collection.[21] In 1913, the trustees of the museum voted to terminate its association with the Fund, citing the Field Museum as a more appropriate institution to involve itself in archaeological excavation.[22]

In 1892, Hutchinson and Ryerson, with funds augmented by Henry H. Getty, traveled to Egypt to sightsee and to buy works for the museum. They assembled the beginnings of a representative collection including jewelry, amulets, a boat model, and a mummy coffin (see fig. 6).[23] Their sources ranged from the German consul at Luxor to Emil Brugsch, Bey of Gizeh. The museum's register notes that two objects were "taken from a tomb by Mr. H." at Assisot.[24] While this practice was not strictly legal, it was commonplace among tourists.

It was the arrival of James H. Breasted at the University of Chicago that accounts for the high quality of the Art Institute's Egyptian collection before Breasted's

FIGURE 5. Julius Gari Melchers (American, 1860–1932). *Portrait of Charles L. Hutchinson*, 1902. Oil on canvas; 101.7 x 99.2 cm. The Art Institute of Chicago, Gift of Charles L. Hutchinson (1902.105). Note the Greek vase in the background of this portrait.

own efforts at the Oriental Institute led Art Institute trustees to withdraw from the competition of acquisition and yield the field to the Oriental Institute. Yet, from 1894 to 1920, with Breasted's guidance, the museum continued to buy, the first purchase being the entire collection of the Reverend Chauncey Murch, the head of the American Mission in Luxor.[25] Included in the collection were hundreds of scarabs (symbolic stone beetles) representing most of the dynasties of Egypt. These were published in 1906 after careful research by Breasted and G. C. Pier.[26] Another associate from the University of Chicago, George Corliss, was offered $75 a month to classify and arrange the exhibit of new material in the museum's new building.

The World's Columbian Exposition of 1893 brought with it a plethora of Neoclassical buildings made of plaster, as well as the Art Institute's present building that features a reproduction of the Parthenon frieze on its north and south facades. The classical collection, both casts and original works, dominated the new museum building. The peregrinations of the ancient art collection around the Art Institute's galleries reveal the museum's changing focus. In the 1890s, the Art Institute was installed and an illustrated guide was organized to provide the public with a course in art history, depending heavily on

FIGURE 6. Installation of ancient Egyptian collection at the Art Institute, 1901. This photograph of a corner of the museum's Egyptian Room reveals the remarkable profusion and variety of Egyptian works in the Art Institute's collection. Photo: The Art Institute of Chicago, *General Catalogue of Paintings, Sculpture, and Other Objects of Art in the Museum, August, 1901*, n. pag.

reproductions, which filled the first floor (see fig. 1). In 1899, when a group of reproductions of bronzes from Pompeii were acquired, they were installed next to, but not mingled with, the Greek and Roman artifacts housed in a prominent gallery on the first floor. By 1922, the Greek vases occupied the present location of the Museum Shop, and the Egyptian material filled part of the present Prints and Drawings galleries. The Art Institute's no longer extant Blackstone Hall housed the cast collection. In the 1940s, the bulk of the Egyptian holdings first moved to a basement gallery and then to the Oriental Institute. The dispersal of the cast collection began in the 1940s, making room for the installation of the Robinson glass collection next to the Greek and Roman holdings. Finally, in the 1960s, with the last of the plaster casts disposed of, a selection of the classical and Egyptian material was installed on the second floor, around the Grand Staircase in the Henry Crown Gallery.

Although ancient art had dominated the early accessions, at the century's end the museum's ambitions expanded to encompass all periods of art. The glory days of buying antiquities wholesale were over. The collection became a more passive recipient of donors' largesse, which fortunately included some of Martin Ryerson's astute purchases. For instance, in 1907, Ryerson gave a group of vases (including cat. no. 25) to the museum that he had bought at the famous Van Branteghem sale in Paris in 1892.[27] This group included three handsome white-ground lekythoi (oil bottles), one by the Achilles Painter (cat. no. 28).

Although the museum had received a smattering of ancient coins from assorted collectors, it was Mr. William F. Dunham's gift of 700 Greek and Roman coins of the highest quality that created the core of an ever-growing collection. When divorced from their numismatic role, these coins are superb examples of low relief and, like intaglios and cameos, they reveal the miniaturist sculptor's skill.

Dunham's gift was accepted by the museum contingent on his buying and donating a safe for its storage. Having met this condition, Dunham asked if his collection was ever going to be displayed. The directors of the museum "stated that if he would build a concrete and steel vault with walls about 26" thick and have a trust fund of $30,000, that they would then be able to. . .place the collection on view."[28] Although Dunham demurred, he continued to give coins and medals to the museum and was appointed "Honorary Curator of Metallic Art" in 1923.[29] Within the next two years, Ryerson and Mrs. William N. Pelouze added their coin collections to this core, providing the museum with a rich series of small works that serve as sociological and historical comments on the larger works in the collection.

For reasons unstated in the minutes, the trustees decided in 1919 to enlarge the Egyptian collection, and they voted to appropriate $5,000 so that Professor Breasted could purchase "Egyptian objects of artistic interest during his trip abroad."[30] Breasted clearly enjoyed his assignment; his talents combined deep erudition with a discriminating eye and an enviable proximity to the sources of supply. He knew and was trusted by the Cairo antiquities dealers. In the Art Institute's name, he made the largest number of purchases from Maurice Nahman, whom he described to his friend, Charles Hutchinson, as follows:

Nahman is a wealthy Syrian, first cashier of the Credit Foncier, and lives in a palatial house with a huge drawing room as big as a church, where he exhibits his immense collection.[31]

Nahman sold Breasted three relief fragments from Old Kingdom mastaba tombs and an exquisite limestone relief of a quail chick used as an artist's model or votive plaque. From other dealers Breasted bought more "artist's models" (such as cat. no. 13), a rare and splendid granite portrait head from the Thirteenth Dynasty (cat. no. 4), and a delicate drawing of a pharaoh.

The Art Institute trustee minutes of December 26, 1919, show that Breasted urged the museum to double its purchase budget.[32] Breasted noted two objects in particular in his list of available acquisition: a relief characterized as "one of the finest pieces I ever saw" (cat. no. 3)[33] and a bronze figure of Anubis, the jackal god (cat. no. 10), that he described as "a magnificent piece."[34] In a letter to Hutchinson, he described his Herculean effort on behalf of the Art Institute:

These pieces were bought by Dr. Gordon, director of the Philadelphia Museum, but he is not an orientalist and he has now written Blanchard (the dealer) with such uncertainty about them, that Blanchard regards himself as released. . . . An hour ago I learned of this and mounting a borrowed bicycle for lack of other conveyance. . . , I rode as fast as I could to Blanchard's place. I saved the bronze by only a few minutes, for Colonel Samuels, a wealthy British officer, was just about to pay the money. . . . As for the superbly colored relief, it will be snapped up the minute the Metropolitan Museum people see it, and they are expected hourly, for they have landed in Alexandria.[35]

The museum's unusual agent "took the plunge" and bought both pieces in the Art Institute's name. They are two of the most beautiful examples in the Egyptian collection. In the 1940s, because of the success of Breasted's Oriental Institute at the University of Chicago, the museum's trustees sent most of the Egyptian collection on a long-term loan to the Oriental Institute, where it has been studied and displayed. In 1993, fifty Egyptian objects were recalled from the Oriental Institute for installation in the Art Institute's new galleries of ancient art.

During the 1920s, Theodore W. Robinson, a successful Chicago businessman, began to buy Roman glass vials and bowls. His interest blossomed into a true collector's passion. Ten years later, as abruptly as he had begun, he stopped collecting. Yet, within that decade, he gathered a body of ancient glass that represents most forms and techniques of glassmaking in the ancient world. A meticulous record keeper, Robinson's archive reflects an elegant world in which dealers in New York, London, and Jerusalem trustingly shipped off cases of glass on approval, hoping to tempt their client with the seductive surfaces and rare shapes of early glass. One year into his new hobby, Robinson noted that "this new fad of mine I find really running into more money than I had anticipated,"[36] but he continued to buy. In the best collecting tradition he educated himself in his new passion, recognizing fakes easily and asking for source information from his dealers. He traced one of his finest pieces, a kohl container from eighteenth-dynasty Egypt (cat. no. 58), to the nineteenth-century collection of Hackey Bey, director of the Constantinople Museum.[37] With the onset of the Great Depression, Robinson stopped buying glass, and between 1941 and 1949 he gave his 519 works to the Art Institute.

With the deaths of Hutchinson in 1924 and Ryerson in 1932, the aggressive acquisition of ancient art dwindled to occasional purchases, but these have been of exceptionally high quality. In the late 1920s, three pieces of large-scale sculpture entered the collection, perhaps because a formal Committee on Egyptian and Classical Art was formed with Alfred Hamill as its chairman.[38] His gift of a Roman relief showing a portion of the Athena Parthenos's shield (cat. no. 48) was bought from a dealers' show mounted at the museum in hopes of stimulating donations as well as encouraging private collecting. A large Attic grave stele and a lovely fragmentary copy of a torso in the Praxitelean style (cat. no. 34) were the only pieces of original sculpture bought for the collection until recent decades. With the retirement of the plaster-cast collection in the 1940s and 1950s, large-scale sculpture was the collection's most glaring lacuna, a lack that was not filled until 1972 when Suzette Morton Davidson gave the museum a full-figure statue of Meleager (cat. no. 41), a Roman copy of a statue by the Greek sculptor Skopas. Purchases have provided a full-scale copy of Praxiteles's *Aphrodite of Knidos* (cat. no. 50) and a series of Roman portrait heads including a lively marble head of the emperor Hadrian (cat. no. 47).

Few individuals have had more influence on the ancient art collection than David Adler, whose gift was not objects but a princely endowment. Adler was a prominent architect whose houses, built for Chicago's elite, are still noted for their careful detail and satisfying proportions. In light of his later commitment to ancient art, it is interesting to note that during his first year at Princeton one of Adler's few passing grades was in ancient Greek. His interest in classicism expanded during his training at the Ecole des Beaux-Arts in Paris.[39] When his beloved wife Katherine died in a car accident in France at the age of thirty seven, Adler conceived of an fund named for her, which continues to enrich the Art Institute's collection to this day.

Many individual donors have enriched the collection according to their particular tastes and interests.

Roman mosaics from Syria were given by Mr. and Mrs. Robert B. Mayer, who bought the group from a dealer on condition that they eventually be given to a museum.[40] In addition to gifts of handsome decorative arts in the form of lamps, mirrors, and small statuettes, the Alsdorf Foundation provided the collection with its most avidly researched object—a sarcophagus fragment picturing Meleager and/or Alexander the Great (cat. no. 55). Robert Grover has added to the coin holdings with his donation of an enormous collection of coins minted by the Romans in Egypt and Asia Minor (such as cat. no. 14).

During the 1970s and 1980s, when the collection was managed first by Patrice Marandel, then by Louise Berge Robertson and Jack Sewell, significant acquisitions were again made. These acquisitions concentrated on sculpture, but the museum acquired vases, as well. Geometric pottery was introduced to the collection with a four-horse pyxis (cat. no. 19) and an imposing serving dish-on-stand from Italy. A serene Cycladic marble female idol beautifully exemplifies the beginning of stone sculpture in third-millennium Greece (cat. no. 17). The Art Institute purchased an early bronze mirror illustrating a scene from the Trojan War (cat. no. 37) and a polychrome temple antefix of writhing warriors and giants (cat. no. 39) to supplement its scanty Etruscan holdings. To represent Greek potters in southern Italy, Robertson acquired five splendid vases (including cat. no. 35) that show the vigorous affluence of the Greek colonies in Italy. Two additional gifts, small in size but large in significance, are a Geometric bronze fibula given by the staff of the museum and a fifth-century B.C. handle from a bronze pot given by the collection's support group, the Classical Art Society. These donations bespeak the renewed interest in all things classical, which is evident one hundred years after Chicago's first burst of classical frenzy.

The formation of the ancient art collection at the Art Institute is the result of both vigorous enthusiasm and discerning taste. The Hutchinson, Ryerson, and Breasted symbiosis created the underpinnings of the collection upon which donors of objects and funds have generously built. As the only comprehensive collection representing the arts of the ancient Mediterranean world on view in Chicago, the Art Institute's collection reflects the aim of its founders: to display the variety and richness of craftsmanship that served as the matrix for subsequent Western art.

Egyptian Art

EMILY TEETER

Assistant Curator
Oriental Institute Museum
University of Chicago

Egyptian art reflects one of the most enduring artistic traditions of the ancient world. Although there were modifications in the style of Egyptian art during the 3,000 years when pharaohs ruled the Nile Valley, objects from any period of this time are instantly recognizable as being of Egyptian origin.

The permanence of Egypt's artistic tradition can be traced to the function of its art. Virtually all examples of two-dimensional work—whether wall painting or carved relief—and all examples of statuary and architecture are related in some way to religious beliefs pertaining to Egyptian mortuary cults or to the veneration of the gods and kings. Indeed, the kinds of objects that are encountered in museum galleries and that fill art reference books were thought to be able to transcend the barriers of temporal existence and go beyond the restraints of life and death. The belief in the potency of art dictated that the mere representation of foodstuffs within the tomb was capable of sustaining the soul of the deceased in the afterlife. The image of an individual, carved in imperishable stone and incised with names and titles, served to perpetuate that person among the living for eternity. Very few examples of Egyptian art existed for purely aesthetic reasons.

The Western conception of equating change with positive progress was unknown in ancient Egypt. On the contrary, the Egyptians believed that the condition of the world was perfect at the time of creation and that earlier styles were to be carefully preserved and emulated. This innate conservatism ran deep in the Egyptian psyche. Rituals and beliefs that the art served, such as the belief that rebirth was dependent upon the preservation of a representation of the deceased, were firmly established at an early date. Since art served the needs of stable religious beliefs, the themes and forms of Egyptian art were particularly resistant to change.

In practical terms, the uniformity of Egyptian art was the result of a common proportional system that employed guide lines and grids. For example, from the time of the Old Kingdom (c. 2700 B.C.), the standing human figure was proportioned from the hairline to the soles of the feet by an eighteen-square grid (see illustration on p. 16). Likewise, the length of the foot was allotted three squares, while the torso from neck to waist spanned four squares. This system was maintained until the Twenty-Fifth Dynasty (c. 700 B.C.), after which time the grid was modified to twenty-one squares, a change that resulted in the elongation of the figures prominent in Ptolemaic and Roman era art (c. 332 B.C.–A.D. 395).

Continuity in artistic styles was also ensured by the existence of workshops in which the official representations of the king and deities were produced under the supervision of temple or palace officials. Each work was the product of many artisans. Not only were they specialized by specific task, such as painting or carving, but master craftsmen did the most complicated section of compositions, leaving routine work to apprentices. As a result of this teamwork, few pieces of Egyptian art can be attributed to an individual artist, and fewer yet are signed.

The conventions of ancient Egyptian art distinguish it from the products of other ancient and modern cul-

FACING PAGE: *Wall Fragment from the Tomb of Amenemhet and His Wife Hemet*, Middle Kingdom, Dynasty 12 (c. 1991-1784 B.C.) (detail of cat. no. 3).

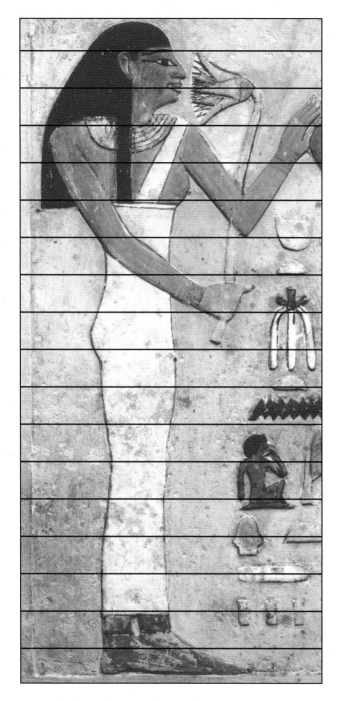

ABOVE: The human form was drawn using a strict system of measurement that divided the body, from the hairline to the soles of the feet, into eighteen equal parts. In this system, the length from the waist to the baseline was always eleven units, while the torso and head was seven, resulting in the uniform long-legged, high-waisted appearance of Egyptian figures. In the eighth century B.C., the system was expanded to twenty-one units, resulting in even more elongated figures.

tures. Its apparent ambiguities may even seem childlike to those who are the inheritors and perpetuators of Western artistic traditions, for Egyptian art is emphatically non-Western. The distinctive conventions of Egyptian art have been referred to as "conceptual" rather than "perceptual," thereby stressing that each subject was portrayed as if in isolation. Each of the essential and identifying characteristics of the subject was portrayed, and each object was represented not from the frame of reference of the viewer, but from the object itself. Hence, foreshortening, inherent in the Western tradition of perspective, was never adopted by Egyptian artists because it was thought to distort the essential form of the subject. Overlapping was avoided to prevent masking essential characteristics of individual objects in complex compositions. An object that was acknowledged to be behind another did not diminish in size as in Western art, but was rather placed above the nearer object to show both forms.

The representation of the human form likewise served to stress essential data about the subject. The shoulders are nearly in frontal view to show the width of the body and not obscure the far arm, while the chest was represented in profile to show its contour. The legs are shown laterally to portray the form of the feet and to indicate rest or movement. With few exceptions, forehead, nose, and chin are in profile to emphasize contour, while the eye is portrayed frontally, to clearly show the pupil in a non-abstracted manner. Most examples of Egyptian representations of humans are heavily idealized and cannot be said to be portraiture. The portrayals strive to depict the individual as eternally slim, youthful, and healthy, for this was the image that he or she wished to maintain for eternity.

The legacy of Egyptian art is difficult to assess. The Sahara Desert prevented significant contact between the Nile Valley and central African civilizations. Certainly, much Egyptian influence can be seen in the arts of Nubia (modern Sudan and southern Egypt), just as Nubian influence can be seen in Egyptian art. The question of interchange between Egyptian and Greek artistic cultures has been impacted by recent linguistic studies that suggest that in the Ptolemaic era (332–30 B.C.) the two cultures did not mix substantially. Artisans created Greek-style representations for Greek clients, and Egyptian-style statuary for native Egyptians. Much of the perceived fusion is merely the result of adding Egyptian costumes and trappings to Greek or Roman works of art.

The exotic conventions, the reminder of the existence of a powerful and sophisticated kingdom of great antiquity, and the religious potency of the art and what it tells us about the complex beliefs of these ancient peoples continue to evoke a special and strong attraction to the arts of ancient Egypt in the modern mind.

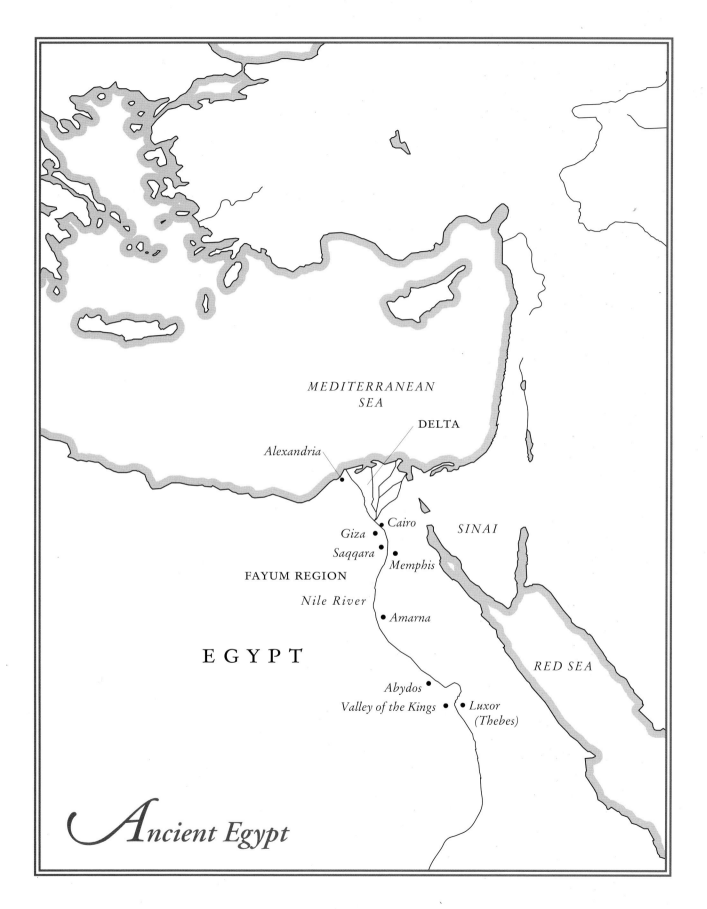

MEDITERRANEAN
SEA

DELTA

Alexandria

Cairo

Giza

Saqqara

Memphis

SINAI

FAYUM REGION

Nile River

Amarna

EGYPT

RED SEA

Abydos

Valley of the Kings

Luxor
(Thebes)

Ancient Egypt

1. Wall Fragment from the Tomb of Thenti

This relief fragment from the tomb of the judge and scribe Thenti shows the deceased and his wife sitting on either side of an offering table piled with reed-shaped loaves of bread. Thenti wears the classic knee-length kilt, the belt looped at his waist. His hair or wig is closely cropped and he is clean-shaven. His wife, whose name is now illegible, wears a tight sheath dress that stops just below her breasts. She is ornamented with a beaded necklace, a choker, and bracelets, and a heavy wig composed of a series of braids. Their son, also named Thenti, stands behind his mother. A small girl, whom the hieroglyphic text identifies as Thenti's granddaughter, stands anchored on her own small baseline. She sucks her finger in a gesture traditionally associated with small children in Egyptian art.

This scene displays many features of the classic Egyptian artistic conventions for human representation. The small toes of the near foot, for example, are invisible, the feet being rendered identically. When both feet are visible, as with the younger Thenti, the arch of each foot is visible, as if both were viewed from the inside. Only one of the woman's breasts is portrayed, for her torso is shown in combined profile and frontal views to express simultaneously its width and contour.

The hieroglyphic texts enumerate the offerings that were desired to sustain Thenti and his family in the afterlife. In addition to food, he requests clothing, linen, incense, green and black eye paint, and material used in the embalming process. (ET)

2. Alabaster Vessels

Egyptian alabaster (calcium carbonate or properly calcite or travertine) is a soft stone that was favored throughout Egyptian history for its color and for the fact that it

1. **Wall Fragment from the Tomb of Thenti**
Egyptian
Old Kingdom, Dynasty 5 (c. 2524–2400 B.C.)
Limestone; h. 53.3 cm (21 in.)
Museum Purchase Fund, 1920.265
References: Thomas George Allen, *A Handbook of the Egyptian Collection* (Chicago, 1923), pp. 23 and 26 (ill.).

could be polished to a high gloss. Alabaster was available in a wide variety of colors, from bright white to
yellow and even nearly to green, usually with contrast-
ing bands of white. Found mainly in Egypt's Eastern
Desert, alabaster was used for large-scale architectural
features (floors, columns, walls, shrines), statues and stelae, and small objects. The material was worked with
copper chisels, saws, and drills, and it was smoothed
with pebbles and possibly scraps of leather. The workmanship of alabaster vessels shows great variation. While
the walls of some vessels are so thin as to be translucent,
some of the smaller squat vessels have only a tiny interior cavity whose shape has little relationship to its exterior profile. Unfinished examples indicate that the outside of a vessel was generally completed before the
interior was hallowed out.

Alabaster was most commonly employed for small-
scale luxury vessels such as those shown here. The tall
flaring beaker, for example, which was used for food
and liquid offerings, is characteristic of the early Old
Kingdom Period. Shorter covered pots of the same general shape were intended for cosmetic or funerary oils.

Squat jars with a narrow neck and a flat wide rim, usually equipped with a disk lid, were designed to hold kohl, a copper-based eye paint used by both men and women. Egyptian artisans also employed alabaster to make open bowls and vases. (ET)

3. Wall Fragment from the Tomb of Amenemhet and His Wife Hemet

This fragment from a tomb chapel portrays the official Amenemhet and his wife Hemet standing before funerary offerings. He wears a pleated white kilt with an inverted pleat that is depicted as a triangular projection. The low table before him is heaped with reed-shaped loaves of bread, a haunch of beef, and vegetables. To the right of the table stands a nested basin and ewer, and three tall vessels for liquid offerings. According to the conventions of Egyptian art, the vegetables and calf's head shown above the jars are considered to be behind them. The small figure to the upper right, also named Amenemhet, presents a haunch of beef to the deceased.

Amenemhet's wife Hemet stands behind her husband, her hand affectionately on his shoulder. She holds a flower to her nose, an allusion to rebirth in the afterlife. In typical Old Kingdom style, the skin of Hemet is colored yellow, while the skin of her husband is a ruddy red. The well preserved pigment is a good reminder that most Egyptian monuments were originally brightly colored.

This relief from Amenemhet's tomb chapel served to immortalize him and his family for eternity through the preservation of their images, names, and food offerings. The hieroglyphic text calls upon the god Osiris to grant them sustenance in the afterlife. This scene was originally located above the tomb's "false door," a representation of a portal that allowed the spirit of the deceased access from the subterranean burial chamber into the decorated tomb chapel. (ET)

4. Head of an Official

This nearly life-sized head of a man—a fragment of a once complete statue—exemplifies the art of the late Middle Kingdom. The face shows careful modeling in the expressive mouth, well-defined upper lip, and eye sockets. The large ears, which are characteristic of much Middle Kingdom sculpture, are slanted slightly backwards and are schematic, with no detailing of the outer ear. The cheekbones are high, while the sides of the face are nearly unmodeled flat planes. The eyebrows are indicated by pecking rather than with the more common carved or relief line. The conventional style of the wig features the thick locks tucked behind the ears, falling to blunt-cut triangular points upon the shoulders.

The financial resources needed to commission a statue of this size and quality suggests that the man whom it portrays was an official of some circumstance. It may have been produced for his tomb where it would have symbolically partaken of the offerings left for the main-

4. **Head of an Official**
Egyptian
Middle Kingdom, Dynasty 13
(c. 1783 B.C.)
Black granite; h. 33.8 cm (13¾ in.)
Museum Purchase Fund, 1920.261
References: Allen, *A Handbook of the Egyptian Collection,* p. 51 (ill.).

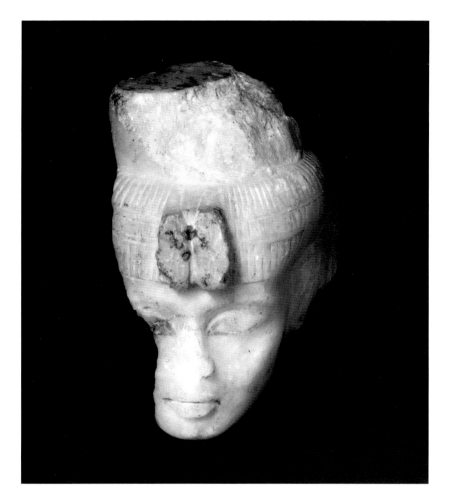

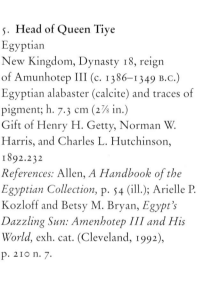

5. **Head of Queen Tiye**
Egyptian
New Kingdom, Dynasty 18, reign
of Amunhotep III (c. 1386–1349 B.C.)
Egyptian alabaster (calcite) and traces of
pigment; h. 7.3 cm (2⅞ in.)
Gift of Henry H. Getty, Norman W.
Harris, and Charles L. Hutchinson,
1892.232
References: Allen, *A Handbook of the
Egyptian Collection,* p. 54 (ill.); Arielle P.
Kozloff and Betsy M. Bryan, *Egypt's
Dazzling Sun: Amenhotep III and His
World,* exh. cat. (Cleveland, 1992),
p. 210 n. 7.

tenance of the soul of the deceased.

Like other relatively hard stone statues, this black granite head was produced with stone tools. Pounders and stone picks would have been used to rough out the basic form, and smoothing and polishing stones were used to finish it. Most stone statues were originally painted in lifelike tones. (ET)

5. Head of Queen Tiye

This fragment of a small statue depicts the head of a woman with pierced ears, and a heavy striated wig. A pair of protective uraeui—the sacred cobras that were emblems of Egyptian royalty—hang from the fillet encircling her head. The head has a full and sensuous lower lip, with down-turned edges to the mouth. The broad nose is now badly damaged. The slender almond-shaped eyes and the eyebrows are delineated with pigment.

The date of this masterfully carved fragment can be deduced from its iconography and style. The use of the double uraeus on the forehead of a queen is rare. It is known from representations of a few New Kingdom Queens including Ahmose Nofertari, Tiye, and Nefertiti of the Eighteenth Dynasty, and Nofertari, wife of Ramesses the Great of the Nineteenth Dynasty. The full lips and down-turned edges of the mouth, as well as the slender almond eyes argue for a late New Kingdom date, during the Amarna Period (c. 1349–1335 B.C.). Although the headdress is badly damaged, the flat top and outline suggest that it was a platform crown, which is most frequently seen on representations of Queen Tiye, the mother of King Akhenaton. (ET)

6. Shawabty of Nebseni

A shawabty (also called a *ushebti*) is a mummiform statuette that was thought to be able to serve the deceased in the afterlife. Here, the simplified rendering of the human figure represents the body of Nebseni in his mummy wrappings. This representation, as well as the presence of the false beard, stresses Nebseni's association with the god Osiris, the principal deity of the afterlife.

The finely incised and pigment-filled inscription is

6. **Shawabty of Nebseni**
Egyptian
New Kingdom, early Dynasty 18,
c. 1570 B.C.
Wood (tamarisk) and pigment; h. 28.2 cm
(10¾ in.)
Gift of Henry H. Getty and Charles L.
Hutchinson, 1892.28
References: Allen, *A Handbook of the
Egyptian Collection,* pp. 64 (ill.) and 66n;
G. T. Allen, *The Egyptian Book of the
Dead Documents in the Oriental Institute
at the University of Chicago* (Chicago,
1960), p. 72, pl. CVI.

a version of chapter 6 of the *Book of the Dead,* excerpts from which appear on most other shawabtys as well. The text affirms, in part, that "if [the deceased] be called upon to do any work which needs to be done in the realm of the dead. . .'Here I am' you shall say." Supplies of these funerary figures were placed in tombs, often as many as one for each day of the year, along with a group of thirty-six overseers. Many shawabty statuettes are supplied with representations of seed baskets, picks, and hoes with which to accomplish their duties. Shawabtys appeared in Dynasty 13 (c. 1784 B.C.), and they continued to be a feature of mortuary furnishings through the Ptolemaic era.

The inscription indicates that Nebseni served as a scribe for a woman who held the title "God's Wife," the rank of a priestess who was considered to be married to the god she served. (ET)

7. **Mummy Case of Paankhenamun**

In the Twenty-Second Dynasty (c. 945 B.C.), the use of form-fitting cartonnage shells made of linen or papyrus impregnated with gum came into fashion. These splendidly decorated cases were usually enclosed within a set of one or two nested, wooden, anthropoid coffins. The cartonnage mummy case itself was formed around a tem-

7. Mummy Case of Paankhenamun
Egyptian
Third Intermediate Period, Dynasty 22
(c. 945–715 B.C.)
Cartonnage (gum, linen, and papyrus),
gold leaf, and pigment; h. 170.2 cm
(67 in.)
William M. Willner Fund, 1910.238
References: Allen, *A Handbook of the
Egyptian Collection,* pp. 7, 12, 13 (ill.),
14–16, 19n., 69, and 124.

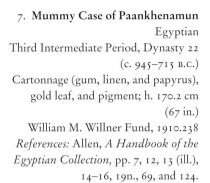

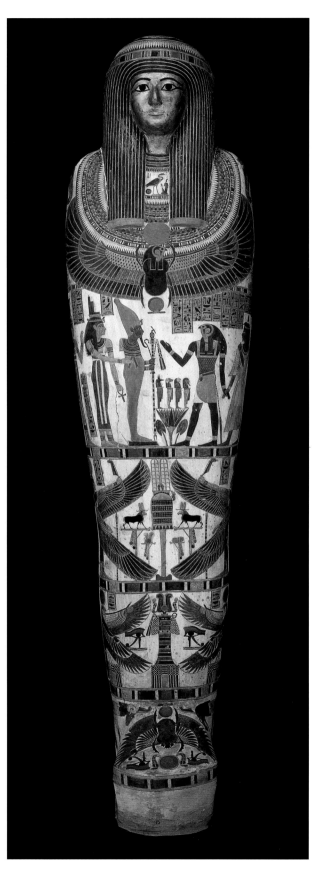

8. **Statuette of Re Horakhty**
Egyptian
Third Intermediate Period, Dynasty
21/25 (c. 1069–656 B.C.)
Bronze and gilt; h. 25 cm (9⅞ in.)
Gift of Henry H. Getty, Charles L.
Hutchinson, and Robert H. Fleming,
1894.261
References: Allen, *A Handbook of the
Egyptian Collection*, pp. 101–02 (ill.);
Günther Roeder, *Agyptische
Bronzefiguren* (Berlin, 1956), pp. 9, 80
(no. 114a), Tafel, 74a.

porary core. A lengthwise seam along the back allowed for the introduction of the wrapped mummy. The seam would then be laced closed and a separate foot board would be inserted at the base. Since the cases are normally coated with a layer of inflexible gesso or plaster, it is assumed that the painted decoration was added after the body was in place. Inserting the wrapped mummy into a finished cartonnage would certainly crack the fragile surface of the shell.

Cartonnage cases are usually painted with symmetrically arranged groupings of protective deities. This example in the Art Institute's collection, made for a doorkeeper in the temple of Amun named Paankhenamun (whose name means "The one who lives for the god Amun"), is decorated with a variety of images associated with rebirth, including the scarab beetle, the hawk-headed god Horus, and a winged solar deity. The largest vignette represents Horus leading the deceased (below the left elbow) into the presence of Osiris, who is attended by his sisters Isis and Nephtyes (see detail, p. 14). A phoenix, the mythical bird associated with rebirth, sits at the throat facing a seated figure of Maat, a goddess who attended the judgement of the deceased. The back of the coffin is decorated with a large *djed* pillar, which represents the backbone of the god Osiris and symbolizes stability. (ET)

9. **Statue of Shebenhor**
Egyptian
Saite Period, Dynasty 26 (c. 664–525 B.C.)
Basalt; h. 28 cm (11 in.)
Gift of Mrs. George L. Otis, 1924.754

8. Statuette of Re Horakhty

This solid cast bronze depicts Re Horakhty, one of the principal deities of the ancient Egyptian pantheon. He is a combination of the gods Re and Horus, both of whom were associated with rebirth. The figure would originally have worn a disk-shaped crown that was inserted into the square hole in the top of his head. A tenon under each foot allowed the statuette to be set upon a separate bronze or wood base. Delicate strokes above the eye imitate the markings of a falcon.

With the exception of the exotic falcon head, the broad chest, defined pectoral muscles, and muscular arms of this figure are characteristic of an idealized representation of an Egyptian in the prime of life. His heavy wig, pleated kilt with knotted belt, heavy beaded broad collar, and even his stance and his prominent navel and nipples emphasize the humanity of this god.

Bronze figures of the gods are rarely encountered prior to the Third Intermediate Period (Dynasty 21, eleventh century B.C.). From that time onward, however, they appear in great numbers and in a staggering variety of themes and sizes. Many of these figures were inscribed with the name of a devotee, who deposited the statue in a temple as evidence of personal piety. The enormous popularity of this practice may be gathered by the discovery of 17,000 such bronzes in a single deposit at the Temple of Karnak in 1903. This particular figure was evidently cherished, for its left foot was broken centuries ago and then repaired. (ET)

9. Statue of Shebenhor

Block-form seated statues first appear in Egypt in the Middle Kingdom (c. 2000 B.C.) and they continue to be popular through the Ptolemaic Period (third to first centuries B.C.). The wide "bag wig," splayed toes, and exaggerated curve of the waist and hips of this statue, as well as the high polish given to its surface, are characteristic of much art of the Late Period (Dynasties 26–31, c. 664–332 B.C.), although the style of this example places it in the early part of the Twenty-Sixth Dynasty. The inscription on the front and back calls upon the gods Osiris and Bastet to give funerary offerings of both Upper and Lower Egypt to Shebenhor, son of Hedebhapiirtbin and Iahchaysnakht.

Intercessory statues such as this were commissioned by individuals to be placed in temples where they would serve as evidence of the piety of the donor. There they would absorb the blessings of the sacred area and transfer them eternally to the owner of the statue. Since the inscription runs off the front surface of the statue, and the roughly hammered text contrasts with the fine finishing of the seated figure, one may conclude that this statue was not commissioned by Shebenhor, but that it was purchased and then inscribed for him. One should not assume, therefore, that this statue makes an effort to be a portrait of the dedicator. The reference to Bastet of Bubastis suggests that the statue may originally have been erected in the temple to that goddess in the Delta. (ET)

10. Statuette of a Jackal

This extremely fine, solid cast bronze depicts a jackal-form god, identified as either Anubis or Wepwawet. The animal's body is slender, its ears erect. The jackal's long thin legs are emphasized by the exaggerated haunches. The snout, too, is long and thin, and the mouth and nose defined. Fine chasing on the body imitates the texture of the animal's fur. The tail, now missing, would have hung straight down from the rear of the figure, an indication that the figure was attached to the edge of a surface.

Both Anubis and Wepwawet were associated with embalming and the protection of the remains of the deceased. From the New Kingdom onward (c. 1570 B.C.), figures of the jackal deity, usually of wood, were attached to the top of funerary shrines or coffins where the image was thought to afford protection to the contents of the

container. Two square holes on the underside of the figure allowed it to be set securely upon such a surface.

Bronze statues of recumbent jackals are very rare. In 1919, James H. Breasted, who purchased this figure for the Art Institute, described it as "a magnificent piece" and "the finest animal figure of its size" that he had ever seen in Egypt. (ET)

11. Coin Showing King Ptolemy I

Coinage was introduced into Egypt through its lively trade contacts with the Greek world and Persia. Egypt had long had a barter economy, but, increasingly, weighed silver became the preferred medium of exchange. The Egyptians became familiar with the coinage of their trading partners, especially favoring the Athenian silver tetradrachms, which were dependable in weight and quality. Coinage began in earnest after the conquest of Egypt by Alexander in 332–331 B.C. His general Ptolemy I struck coins there first in the name of Philip Arrhidaeus, then for Alexander IV, and eventually in his own name as he established his independence. The early coinage adver-

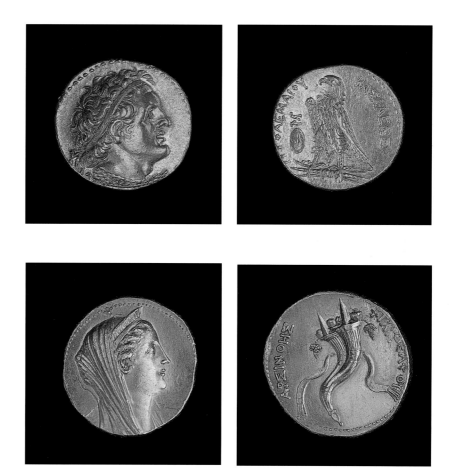

11. Coin Showing King Ptolemy I
Reverse: Eagle on thunderbolt; around,
ΠΤΟΛΕΜΑΙΟΥ ΒΑΣΙΛΕΩΣ
(Ptolemaiou basileos; "[minted by]
Ptolemy, King")
Greek (Alexandria, Egypt)
284–247 B.C. (reign of Ptolemy II),
Cyprus mint
Gold pentadrachm; diam. 2.4 cm (1 in.)
Gift of Martin A. Ryerson, 1922.4933

**12. Coin Showing Queen Arsinoë II,
Deified**
Reverse: Double cornucopia; around,
ΑΡΣΙΝΟΗΣ ΦΙΛΑΔΕΛΦΟΥ
(Arsinoës Philadelphou; "[minted for]
Arsinoë Philadelphos")
Greek (Alexandria, Egypt)
After 270 B.C.
Gold octadrachm; diam. 2.8 cm (1⅛ in.)
Gift of Martin A. Ryerson, 1922.4934

tised Ptolemy's associations with Alexander, but, in time, the new royal dynasty celebrated its confidence with portrait coins of its founders. Ptolemy II and his advisers instituted the ruler-cult honoring the deified Alexander and members of the royal family.

On the obverse ("head") of this coin, the aegis (a magical garment) worn by Ptolemy I alluded to Zeus as well as Athena; it was thought to protect the wearer and repel enemies, and it underscored the divine origins of the dynasty. On the reverse ("tail"), the eagle and the thunderbolt also recall Zeus, with whom, in the form of Zeus-Ammon, the early Ptolemaic dynasty associated itself. (See entry on cat. no. 23 for more information on the "obverse" and "reverse" of ancient coins.) The god Ammon was in residence at the Siwah oasis, and pronounced oracles famous throughout the Greek world. Alexander visited the oasis in 332–331 b.c., where he was greeted by the priests as "son of Zeus," their usual form of address to new pharaohs. (TGD)

12. Coin Showing Queen Arsinoë II, Deified

Queen Arsinoë II, the daughter of Ptolemy I and the sister-goddess-consort of Ptolemy II, is honored on this coin. Several Egyptian pharaohs had been depicted with the ram horn of Amun, and it was adopted by Alexander the Great to advertise his position as son of the god and as the new pharaoh. Despite the strong desire by his Ptolemaic successors to bank on their association with Alexander (Ptolemy I had in fact hijacked Alexander's funeral cortege, with the intention of building a shrine around it at Siwah), none of them adopted the divine horns—with the remarkable exception of Arsinoë (note the outline of the horn beneath her veil). Her use of the lotus-scepter also emphasized that she followed in the footsteps of the pharaohs, and is another indication of the Macedonian-Egyptian political synthesis. Arsinoë was by all accounts a woman of tremendous ambition and political savvy, and she knew what it took to rule

13. Relief Plaque Showing a Queen or Goddess
Egyptian
Ptolemaic Period, 2nd/1st century b.c.
Limestone and traces of pigment;
h. 21.1 cm (8 ¹⁵⁄₁₆ in.)
Museum Purchase Fund, 1920.259
References: Allen, *A Handbook of the Egyptian Collection*, pp. 44–45 (ill.).

14. **Coin Showing Emperor Hadrian**
Obverse: around, AVT KAI TPAI
AΔPIA CEB (Aut[ocrator] Kai[sar]
Trai[anos] Adria[nos] Seb[astos]; "Emperor
Caesar Trajan Hadrian Augustus")
Reverse: Hadrian receives grain from
Alexandria ("Year 15")
Roman (Alexandria, Egypt),
Alexandria mint
A.D. 131
Billion tetradrachm; diam. 2.5 cm (1 in.)
Gift of Robert Grover, 1980.824

her mostly Egyptian subjects. Like Alexander in the East, the Ptolemies adopted many local customs, including the policy of royal-divine marriage of siblings. After her death in 270 B.C., Arsinoë was worshiped as a goddess under the title "Thea Philadelphos." (TGD)

13. Relief Plaque Showing a Queen or Goddess

The woman portrayed on this limestone plaque wears a headdress in the form of a vulture, its wings protectively spread along her head. Bead spacers decorate her elaborate coiffeur, and the ends of her curls are accentuated by tiny drill holes. Rows of lotus flowers, marguerites, and papyrus flowers suspended from a band of round beads compose her broad collar.

The basic features of this work—the woman's general appearance, her headdress, and her jewelry—fit well into a tradition of Egyptian art that spans more than a thousand years. Certain features of this composition, however, are characteristic of the Ptolemaic (Greek) Period in Egypt: specifically the fleshiness of the cheek, chin, and neck; the small almond-shaped eye and the extended eyebrow line; the short rounded nose; and the drilled detail of the wig.

As goddesses, queens, and certain types of priestesses wore the vulture cap headdress, it is impossible to identify the status of the woman depicted. This plaque may have been a sculptor's trial piece, or a votive offering carved to be deposited in a shrine to prove the piety of the dedicant.

Artists of the mid- and late Ptolemaic Period (second to first centuries B.C.) employed a curious artistic convention, evident here, of omitting the broad collar on what we take to be the rear shoulder. This omission probably indicates that that area was considered to be a part of the arm and shoulder, rather than the region of the neck and chest. (ET)

14. Coin Showing Emperor Hadrian

Egypt welcomed the long-awaited visit of Hadrian in A.D. 130, the fifteenth year of his reign. Coins of the fourteenth year had depicted Eirene ("peace") in anticipation of the happy occasion; before Hadrian, Roman emperors typically visited their provinces only in times of wars or insurrections.

The elephant scalp worn by the personification of Alexandria on the reverse of this coin is a reference to the African forest elephant, native to Ethiopia and the Red Sea area, which was used by the Ptolemies as a battle mount. By Hadrian's day, however, the elephant was no longer used in warfare, though it was popular in parades and ceremony, and conjured up days of Egypt's military splendor. Alexandria's gift of wheat to the emperor, which is depicted on the reverse of this coin, signifies Egypt's vast grain exports, on which Rome relied.

Hadrian's idealized portrait is typically philhellene. The artistic style of the Alexandrian mint became more Greco-Roman as a result of Hadrian's interest in the imperial province. Although the coinage of Egypt circulated only within the province, and was not current in the rest of the Empire, the more cosmopolitan look of this coin was meant to convey to Egyptians that Egypt was, after all, a part of Rome. Alexandria had been founded by Alexander the Great, who needed a seaport to Europe; the city *was* the province of Egypt, as far as most Romans were concerned. It remained great until the Arab conquest of A.D. 646 turned Egypt's gaze away from Europe, toward Asia. (TGD)

15. Mummy Head Cover

This covering for the head of a mummy represents a highly idealized image of a woman wearing a heavy wig. The front sections of her hair are braided and orna-

15. **Mummy Head Cover**
Egyptian
Roman Period, 1st century B.C.
Cartonnage (gum, linen, and papyrus),
gold leaf, and pigment; h. 46 cm (18⅛ in.)
William M. Willner Fund, 1910.221
References: Allen, *A Handbook of the
Egyptian Collection*, pp. 16–17 (ill.).

mented with golden beads and rosettes. The fringe of the woman's own hair appears as curls along her forehead. She wears a locketlike ornament in the form of the hieroglyph for "heart." Her chest is covered with the representation of a wide collar made of rows of floral and geometric ornaments. This lower margin is decorated with a scene of Osiris seated on his throne, flanked by a pair of protective deities, and an image of the deceased (shown kneeling) followed by the so-called four sons of Horus, who were associated with the protection of the vital organs of the mummy. Isis and Nephthys, the divine sisters of Osiris who act as mourners for the deceased, appear on the shoulders.

In the Ptolemaic Period (332–30 B.C.), the head, feet, and chest of wrapped mummies were often covered with cartonnage, which was thought to ensure the function of those parts of the body in the afterlife even if the mortal remains were decayed or destroyed. Such cartonnage headpieces are direct descendants of helmet-style masks like the famous gold covering of Tutankhamun (c. 1334 B.C.). Not only did these head coverings provide a substitute for the vital facilities of the head, but the gilt-covered surface of the mask also served to identify the deceased with the sun god Re, whom the Egyptians described as having skin of gold. (ET)

16. **Mummy Portrait**

The belief that rebirth in the afterlife was dependent upon the preservation of the body, or of an image of the deceased, was adopted by the Roman population of Egypt. The trappings of these beliefs, however, were modified to meet contemporary tastes. During the Roman Period, the idealized cartonnage head covers (see cat. no. 15) were abandoned in favor of portraits painted in tempera or in encaustic (molten wax) on board. These portraits were secured over the face of the mummy by the linen bandages, damage from which can be seen at the bottom of this panel.

Generally referred to as "Fayum portraits" after the region that first yielded a major find of them, these paintings show the deceased in a very lifelike manner. Diverging from traditional Egyptian art, the painter of this work has positioned the head and torso so that they are not restricted to rigid and formal poses. Instead, the face is turned three-quarters toward the viewer. The heavy lids, arched eyebrows, narrow chin, bowed lips, and beard seek to capture the actual appearance of the individual. As an indication of the strength of traditional iconography, the wreath of ivy in the man's hair is not a Roman fashion, but a reminder of Egyptian funerary scenes in which the convolvulus ivy was associated with rebirth.

These portraits were sometimes painted during the lifetime of the individual, for scraps found among funerary wrappings indicate that some finished panels were cut down to fit the mummy bundle. Several portraits have been discovered in frames, suggesting that they were hung in homes during the lifetime of the individual. (ET)

16. **Mummy Portrait**
Egyptian
Roman Period, 2nd century A.D.
Encaustic (wax and pigment) on wood;
h. 36.8 cm (14½ in.)
Gift of Mrs. Emily Crane Chadbourne,
1922.4798
References: Allen, *A Handbook of the Egyptian Collection,* pp. 161–62 (ill.); Klaus Parlasca, *Mumienporträts und verwandte Denkmäler* (Wiesbaden, 1966), pp. 42, 176n.; *Bulletin of The Art Institute of Chicago* (Nov.-Dec. 1978), vol. 72, no. 6, pp. 1–4.

Greek Art

JOHN GRIFFITHS PEDLEY
Professor of Classical Archaeology
University of Michigan

When contemplating the character of Greek art, many people will think immediately of Athens, and of the great sculptural program that decorated the Parthenon. Or they will think perhaps of the numerous statues of standing male and female figures with which Greeks adorned their sanctuaries, cemeteries, and other public places. Some of these statues, both in marble and bronze, have survived in Greece, and are the prize possessions of the museums where they may now be seen. Others were carried off by Roman conquerors to Italy where they were highly valued, and some were copied or adapted by contemporary artists. Accordingly, much of what we know of Greek art comes from Roman interest and through Roman interpretations. It is Athens of the fifth century B.C., however, and sculpture that spring primarily to mind when Greek art is discussed. But this is not the whole story, whether in terms of chronology, geography, materials, or art forms.

Greek art flourished in the Bronze Age (c. 3000–c. 1100 B.C.), most spectacularly in the abstract female marble figures of Cycladic origin, and after the Dark Age (c. 1100–c. 900 B.C.), when it came to life again under the influence of Egypt and the East. Athens was already a power to be reckoned with, particularly in terms of vase painting, but in the period from circa 900 to circa 600 B.C. other places––such as Euboea and Corinth—stand alongside Athens as significant centers of artistic production. The Archaic (c. 600–c. 480 B.C.)

and Classical (c. 480–c. 323 B.C.) periods witnessed the rise and decline of Athens. The artistic culmination was reached of course in the architecture and sculpture of the fifth-century buildings on the Acropolis. Following the conquests of Alexander the Great, elements of Greek art permeated the known world with new centers of production and consumption in the great capital cities like Egyptian Alexandria. This period is known as the Hellenistic (c. 323–c. 31 B.C.), so called because of the dissemination of Greek (Hellenic) ideas throughout the lands of Alexander's empire.

Greek sculpture flourished in the round, in free-standing reliefs, and in architectural formats; artists worked in limestone, marble, bronze, other metals, bone, ivory, terracotta, and more exotic media (like faience), and combinations such as gold and ivory. Other artists, whose names we know from the literary record, were painters. They painted walls and they painted panels, and they were held in high regard by later writers; so it is all the more disappointing that almost nothing of their work has survived. In contrast, much work of vase painters has come down to us, and some may offer clues as to what larger panels and murals looked like.

Painted vases have survived in large numbers, not least because many were placed in tombs as gifts for the dead, and have been excavated by archaeologists. They yield invaluable information on many aspects of Greek life. Their various uses as storage, pouring, cooling, or drinking vessels are now well understood, while their patterns of distribution indicate important trade connections between city-states. The painted scenes tell much about social life, about customs, beliefs, and religious rites, as well as about the Greek myths. Some

FACING PAGE: *Amphora (Storage Jar)*, 550/525 B.C. (detail of cat. no. 20).

exemplify the concern with representing space, narrative, and the human figure that permeated Greek art.

The problem of representing the third dimension in space was one of the reasons why Athenian vase painters switched from the black-figure to the red-figure technique toward the end of the sixth century B.C. With the increased flexibility offered by the brush, the painter could render foreshortening of forms, three-quarter views of figures, the human body in motion, and moving garments more realistically. During the fifth century, artists continued to experiment with the surface of the vase; for example, wavy groundlines painted up and down the vase supported figures in various postures and suggested spatial distancing. This practice was begun in Athens, and was exploited widely by Greek vase painters in southern Italy in the fourth century.

Narrative elements occur early in vase painting in the Geometric Period (c. 900–c. 700 B.C.). The stories told on these vases seem to be generic representations of situations—of a shipwreck or a combat, for example—without alluding to specific events. They are precursors to the rise of mythological tales loaded with symbolic meaning, which were especially exploited by Athenian vase painters (but also by others) in the seventh and sixth centuries B.C. This practice continued in vase painting through the fourth century, and appeared in other media. Programs of architectural sculpture, for example, were rich in narrative, compressed into a pediment or presented serially in a frieze, and they played their part in informing, teaching, warning, and manipulating those who saw them.

The representation of the human figure was a special concern. Sculptors in the Cyclades of the third millennium B.C. saw the figure, male or female, through an abstract lens. And human figures took on two-dimensional, sticklike shapes on their reappearance during the Geometric Period. Human shapes, however, became increasingly realistic in painting and sculpture; by the fifth century, artists were able to render anatomy accurately, as well as certain varieties of human emotion, character, age, and mood. But the tension between abstract and realistic representation was not resolved. The search for ideal form was still a major concern, and the Greek artists' triumph in imposing external order on the representation of nature, in fusing the ideal with the real, was a major achievement of the High Classical Period. From the beginning of the fourth century, however, the balanced forms favored by famous sculptors and theorists like Pheidias and Polykleitos began to be stretched. Ultimately, in Hellenistic times, realism was pushed to extremes; individualized and exaggerated postures, gestures, and expressions became commonplace.

Art was used by the Greeks to beautify the land-scapes of their citadels, cemeteries, and other public places, and to enrich their domestic lives; it was also used to send messages. These messages could be personal and commemorative, as is the case with grave markers that served both to bring the dead to mind and to allude to the wealth and social status of the dead person and his living kin. Or they could be more generic and politico-religious, drawing attention to the myth history of city-states (as in the pedimental sculpture of the Parthenon) or to the successful and paradigmatic struggles of Greek heroes (as in much of Greek vase painting). On occasion, they could be even more obviously political; the sculptural groups of the Tyrannicides dedicated in the Athenian agora served to emphasize both the end of the tyranny and the success of the new democracy, even if the murder itself had been motivated more by homosexual rivalry than by political enthusiasm.

The study of Greek art may justifiably encompass both aesthetic-philosophical and socio-political dimensions. Yet increasingly students pay attention to the socio-political ramifications, and to purpose. Why was a particular image chosen? Who chose it? Who commissioned it? What is the relation between political events and images on vases or in architectural programs? The context has taken on more and more importance. But there is nothing without the "text" (the vase or the statue or the building), which still repays examination as a self-standing work of art, an emblem, in this Greek instance, of human creativity at the dawn of Western civilization.

BLACK SEA

ITALY

ETRURIA

CORSICA

Cerveteri

Rome
Cales
Capua
Nola

CAMPANIA

LUCANIA

BRUTTIUM

SARDINIA

*ADRIATIC
SEA*

Canosa

APULIA

Metapontum
Tarentum

MACEDONIA

Pella

THRACE

Byzantium

Troy *Assos*

Cyzicus

ANATOLIA

ASIA MINOR

THESSALY

GREECE

*AEGEAN
SEA*

Tanagra

LYDIA

IONIA

Thebes

BOEOTIA

Ephesus
Knidos

Olympia

PELOPONNESOS

Athens
Corinth

SAMOS

Antioch

SICILY

Carthage

Syracuse

Akragas

AEGINA

KEROS

KOS

RHODES

Arsinoe

SYRIA

CYPRUS

CYCLADIC ISLANDS

CRETE

Alexandria

Jerusalem

Nile River

EGYPT

Thebes

The Greek World

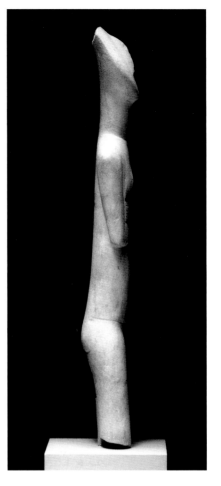

17. Female Figure
Greek (Cycladic Islands, probably from the island of Keros)
Early Bronze Age, 2600/2400 B.C.
Marble; h. 39.6 cm (15¾ in.)
Katherine K. Adler Fund, 1978.115
References: Pat Getz-Preziosi, "The 'Keros Hoard': Introduction to an Early Cycladic Enigma," *Antidoron Jürgen Thimme* (Karlsruhe, 1982), pp. 37–44; Getz-Preziosi, *Early Cycladic Art in North American Collections,* exh. cat. (Richmond, Va., 1989), nos. 26–58 and 73–87, esp. no. 38, pp. 176–77; Jack L. Davis, "Cycladic Figure in Chicago and the Non-Funeral Use of Cycladic Marble Figures," *Cycladia* (London, June, 1983), pp. 15–21, figs. 1–2.

17. Female Figure

Shaped from a block of island marble, this female figure is characteristic of the sculpture of the Cyclades in the third millennium B.C. There is some damage to the nose and the top of the head, and the lower legs were broken off from above the knee and are lost. The local crystalline marble, which splits easily, encouraged the development of a simple style that the conservatism of artisans and users maintained for 500 years. The forms of this sculpture are uncompromisingly abstract: the face is an oval tilted back, the nose a pronounced ridge, and the neck a cylinder. The folded arms are rendered schematically, with only shallow incision articulating fingers, while the abdomen and thighs are long with simple, almost shapeless contours. In profile, the whole figure is strikingly flat and thin. Details of the eyes, mouth, ears, and hair were probably added in paint.

The female figure was, by far, the most popular subject of this style, although other themes included musicians and male warriors. These sculptures have been found mostly in graves, but also in domestic settings. The context of the so-called "Keros hoard," from which this piece is thought to have come, continues to be debated. So the specific function of these figures remains puzzling, although they evidently enjoyed use both in life and death. Were they images of respected ancestors? Or heroines? Or deities? Whatever their creators had in mind, the enthusiasm for representational art that they embody was the special strength of Cycladic artistic production in the third millennium B.C., and this skill distinguished the islands culturally both from contemporary Crete and mainland Greece. (JGP)

18. Pyxis (Container for Personal Objects)

Greece awoke from the monotony of the Geometric Period thanks to stimuli from the east and south. Greek traders had made their way to Syria and Egypt where they encountered new ideas, shapes, and designs. Eastern

18. Pyxis (Container for Personal Objects)
Greek (Corinthian), said to have been found in Attica
Name vase of the Ampersand Painter
580/570 B.C.
Earthenware; h. 14 cm (5⁹⁄₁₆ in.)
Museum Purchase Fund, 1905.343
References: Warren G. Moon, *Greek Vase-Painting in Midwestern Collections,* exh. cat. (Chicago, 1979), pp. 34–35.

and Egyptian objects arrived in Greece and had a profound effect. New techniques of working raw materials produced new kinds of sculpture, architecture, and metallurgy, and new oriental designs changed the face of Greek pottery. These oriental ideas were greeted eagerly in Corinth, which took the lead in introducing new motifs onto the surface of her pots. This pottery, called Protocorinthian for the period from circa 725 to circa 625 B.C., and Corinthian from circa 625 to circa 550 B.C., was popular outside Corinth as well as at home.

The figures on this late Corinthian pyxis were drawn in silhouette and painted black with anatomical details picked out by incision, which allowed the color of the clay to show through. Patches of red and white paint were also used to enliven forms. The technique used here is termed "black-figure." This upright handled pyxis is decorated with a frieze of "panthers," a sphinx, a swan, a doe, and a goat, and the background is filled with so called "splinter" rosettes. As was usual in this Corinthian style, the artist evidently felt a great reluctance to leave any part of the surface of the pot undecorated. The painter of this pyxis is known as the Ampersand Painter because of the lengthened and curving shape he frequently gave to the tail of a sphinx, as here, and its similarity to the ampersand, the symbol often printed for "and." This is his name vase. (JGP)

19. Pyxis (Container for Personal Objects)

This circular box, or pyxis, which was used to contain cosmetics, jewelry, trinkets, or other personal items, was made in Athens in the middle years of the eighth century B.C. Its surface decoration exemplifies the age known as the Geometric Period because of the precise and mathematical style of its painted designs. Athens was the major center of production of Geometric pottery like this, but other centers have been identified.

The surface of both box and lid of this pyxis is decorated in friezes and panels employing standard geometric designs—meanders, checkerboard patterns, dotted and crosshatched lozenges, chevrons, and so forth—rendered in a dark paint on a light ground. The handle of the lid is in the form of four horses presented in the Geometric style (so Geometric can be used to refer either to the period or to the style) with cylindrical bodies, short flat necks, tubular heads, and otherwise flat forms. Horse handles appeared first in Geometric works either as a single horse or a pair, and later in teams of three or four, as here. The presentation of inanimate forms as animate beings either human or animal, as in the handle of this pyxis, is a characteristic trait of Greek art in this and other periods. The horses themselves take on a social significance as emblems of aristocracy, since the raising of horses was an aristocratic pursuit that only the rich could afford. (JGP)

20. Amphora (Storage Jar)

In the course of the seventh century B.C., curvilinear and floral motifs began to appear on Athenian pottery. Athenian vase painters also began to draw scenes with figures on large surfaces using a technique that relied partly on silhouette, which was inherited from the Geometric style, and partly on outline. One great con-

19. **Pyxis (Container for Personal Objects)**
Greek (Attic)
Geometric Period, 760/735 B.C.
Earthenware; h. 28.6 cm (11¼ in.)
Costa A. Pandeleon Fund, 1976.2

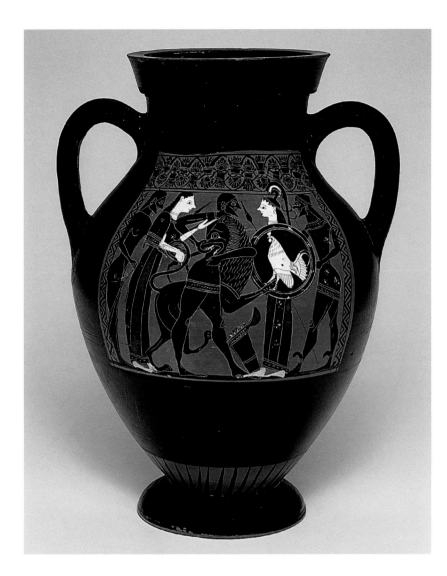

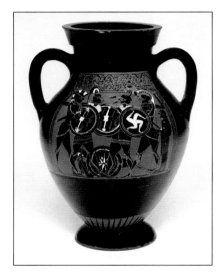

20. **Amphora (Storage Jar)**
Greek (Attic)
The Painter of Tarquinia RC 3984
550/525 B.C.
Earthenware, black-figure technique;
h. 28.2 cm (10¾ in.)
Katherine K. Adler Fund, 1978.114
References: Moon, *Greek Vase-Painting
in Midwestern Collections*, pp. 52–53.

tribution of this Protoattic style was the expansion of the concept of narrative representation. Narrative scenes had appeared on late Geometric pottery and appear to have been generic. But in Attica in the seventh century, scenes from particular myths (Perseus and the Gorgons, for example) and from the epic tradition (Odysseus was especially popular) frequently appeared. This interest in storytelling continued in the sixth century, when vases decorated in the black-figure technique vividly displayed scenes from myth and from the lives of the great Greek heroes.

Such heroic scenes appear in panels on this amphora made in Athens around 550 B.C. Amphorae were used for the transport and storage of such items as wine, olives, and pitch, or as domestic containers, or as prizes for victory in the games. Here, on the front, the struggle between Herakles and the Nemean lion is over; Herakles has a stranglehold on the lion, whose jaws he has pried

open with his bare hands. To one side stand a fully armed Athena and Hermes, identified by his boots, hat and special staff (the *caduceus*); to the other side are a balancing pair of figures, one male and one female. On the back of the amphora, pairs of warriors fight over the body and armor of a fallen comrade or antagonist. (JGP)

21. Hydria (Water Jar)

Another popular shape on which narrative episodes were painted in the black-figure technique was the hydria. Such vases proliferated in the second half of the sixth century B.C., especially after the water-supply in Athens was improved by the construction of fountainhouses and the aqueducts bringing water to them. In fact, several hydriaie of the later years of the century are decorated with images of fountainhouses with women or slaves shown drawing water from them.

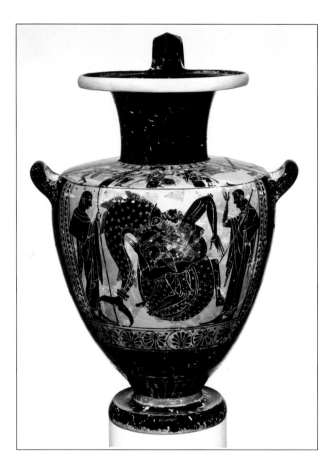

Detail of Shoulder

21. **Hydria (Water Jar)**
Greek (Attic), said to have been found
at Cerveteri, Italy
A painter of the Leagros Group
520/500 B.C.
Earthenware, black-figure technique;
h. 50.1 cm (19¾ in.)
Gift of Philip D. Armour and Charles L.
Hutchinson, 1889.15
References: J. D. Beazley, *Attic Black-
Figure Vase-Painters* (New York, 1978),
p. 673; *Paralipomena* (Oxford, 1971),
p. 164.

This three-handled, flat-shouldered hydria is decorated on the shoulder with three seated and three striding figures, among whom appear Athena and Hermes. On the main panel Herakles (for whom Athena and Hermes were ardent partisans) wrestles with the sea monster Triton, flanked by two bystanders. The intricate composition has the Greek hero astride the monster, his arms locked around Triton's neck in an implacable grip, while Triton flails his arms, black fingers stretched against the red background. They face different directions—Herakles to the viewers' right and up, victorious, and Triton to the left and down, vanquished. Precise incision renders the outline and details of the lion skin that Herakles wears, as well as the contour and detail of Triton's scales and fins. Herakles became a favorite image of the Peisistratid tyranny in Athens, and this particular scene, in fact, of the conquest of the sea monster was used to decorate, in limestone figures, the pediment of a temple built on the Acropolis at Athens in about the middle of the sixth century. (JGP)

22. Amphora (Storage Jar)

The black-figure technique, popular in Corinth in the seventh and sixth centuries and in Athens in the sixth century, ran its course until challenged by the new red-figure technique in Athens around 525 B.C. Other ways of painting pots were also tried in Athens at about this time. White color, used sparingly in black-figure, was now sometimes used for entire figures ("white-figure") against a black background. More lasting, however, was the application of a white slip to the whole vase or only part of it as a surface for figures or ornament. This technique ("white-ground") may have been borrowed from Greek cities on or near the coast of Asia Minor—Chios, for example—where it enjoyed considerable popularity. At first, black figures were painted in silhouette on the white ground; later, black outline figures appeared. One notable innovator was Nikosthenes, who, though firmly grounded in the black-figure technique, experimented both with "white-figure" and "white-ground."

This amphora displays the larger part of the body painted with rich black Attic gloss, with white-ground used on the shoulder and neck. Black palmettes and tendrils are painted on the shoulder, and black-bearded satyr masks, wreathed in ivy tendrils, in outline on the necks. This is an important experimental piece, perhaps by the Antimenes Painter or a member of his circle. The

Detail of Back

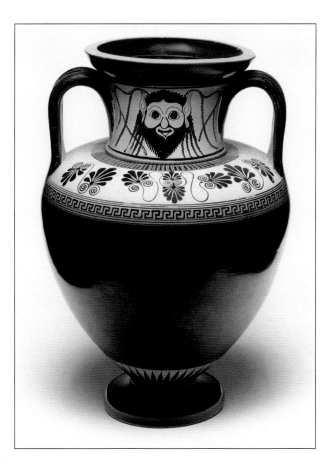

22. **Amphora (Storage Jar)**
Greek (Attic)
Close to the style of the Antimenes
Painter
c. 520 B.C.
Earthenware, black-figure technique;
h. 39.4 cm (15½ in.)
Costa A. Pandeleon Fund, 1980.75
References: The Art Institute of Chicago,
Annual Report 1979–80, p. 31 (ill.).

Antimenes Painter was a fervent practitioner of black-figure during the first years of red-figure at Athens; he is known to have decorated hydriae with white-ground necks. (JGP)

23. Coin Showing the Goddess Athena

The earliest Greek coins usually referred only obliquely to a deity, such as Apollo's lyre on Delian coins, or Artemis's stag at Ephesus. Athens was among the first to put the face of its tutelary goddess on its coins, introducing the type during the reign of the tyrant Hippias (527–510 B.C.). It remained constant, with some few alterations in style, until, centuries later, even the conquering Romans adapted it for use in the province.

The incuse (sunken) field on the reverse is more evidence of the venerable antiquity of the Athenian coinage. The earliest coins were merely blobs or "blanks" of precious metal of a certain weight and purity, which were heated and stamped into an identifying die set into a block or anvil. A punch, with square or round cross-section, was struck with a hammer to force the blank into the die. The resulting coin had a design on the "head" or obverse side (originally a sunken design, soon a relief design) while the "tail" or reverse showed only the round or square outline of the punch. Soon the punch too was decorated with an identifying symbol or words, in this case Athena's owl, but the outline of the punch remained. Advances in die-making technology soon made it possible to get clean strikes on both faces of the coin, with no indication of the punch; but Athens chose to keep its archaic look to emphasize the coinage's unvarying dependability. (TGD)

24. Rhyton (Drinking Vessel) in the Shape of a Donkey Head

The instinct to render inanimate objects as living organisms is a recurrent theme in Greek art. It occurred as early as the Bronze Age when handles of cosmetic boxes were given animal form, and when rhyta (ritual pouring vessels in this period) took the shape of animal heads. These rhyta were made in precious metals or in soft and semiprecious stones for luxury and ritual use in the palatial complexes of Crete and mainland Greece. Much later, during the seventh century, the idea of making terracotta vases in zoomorphic form or with some parts rendered as human or animal shapes returned.

This rhyton is in the shape of the head of a donkey. The name of the potter-coroplast (sculptor in terracotta) is unknown, but the painter was Douris. Calligraphic red-figure palmettes flank the handle on the frieze below the rim, while the figured scene shows a satyr and a maenad (female member of Dionysos's retinue). He is bearded but baldish, with characteristic satyr's ear and tail; she wears old fashioned garments (archaic chiton and transverse himation) and waves a thyrsos. In this period, the rhyton was used as a drinking horn, and thus it would have been appropriate to decorate it with a Dionysiac scene. (JGP)

25. Kylix (Drinking Cup)

Much activity in the potters quarter (the Kerameikos) in Athens was given over to the provision of decorated tableware to be used at symposia (drinking parties). Potters and painters produced vessels for mixing wine and water (kraters), vessels to hold water (hydriaie) or wine (amphorae), and many shapes of drinking cups. This kylix, a shallow drinking cup with horizontal handles, provides a good example of such cups.

The final quarter of the sixth century (c. 525–500 B.C.) had seen much experimentation by artists frustrated by the limitations of the black-figure technique. In their enthusiasm to express emotional states more easily, and to show the human body in more realistic motion, artists turned to the new red-figure technique, in which figures now remained the color of the clay, which in Attica was very malleable, of high quality, and a warm deep orange color when fired.

The exterior of this cup is painted entirely in the glossy black that is characteristic of Athens. On the interior of the cup, Artemis, identified by her attributes (bow, arrows, quiver) strides forward realistically, her swinging folds of drapery following logically the movements of her limbs. Her feet are naturalistically drawn, while her eye is

no longer shown frontally in the profile face, as it had appeared in the black-figure manner. Details of the style of painting of this cup are close to that of Douris (see cat. no. 24), a prolific painter who was active between circa 500 and circa 470 B.C., allowing the conjecture that this is the work of one of his followers. (JGP)

26. Hydria (Water Jar)

In the period after the Persian wars, from circa 475 to circa 450 B.C., some red-figure painters turned away from the novelties of spatial and emotional exploration and looked backward to earlier conventions. Such painters are termed Mannerists, and the painter of this hydria, the Leningrad Painter, was one of them. Space is not explored; the design is on the surface of the pot; gesture and posture count for everything in the theatrical moments portrayed.

Here, a group of five figures stand on a ground line supported by a decorative border. The pair in the middle are the focus of the composition. A garlanded youth with a himation slung around his waist and leaning on a stick in a contrived manner moves toward a girl, putting his left arm around her and grasping suggestively with his right hand toward her groin. She tilts her face towards his, puts her right arm around his neck, and seems ready to caress his ear with her left hand. They seem about to kiss. Such scenes of intimacy are not common, although there are parallels to even the more unusual details on contemporary vases. The embroidery frame lends a domestic flavor to the scene, but the walking sticks suggest that the lads have come from elsewhere and are not at home; so we are more likely in the realm of sexual adventure than that of emotional involvement. (JGP)

27. Stamnos (Wine Jar)

The painted scene on the front of this stamnos, or wine

jar, shows three female figures. To the left, a woman shown in profile view holds up a vase that has the same shape as the stamnos itself. The central figure prepares to place a garland around the vase's neck. She stands in front of a table on which sit a kantharos (a high-handled, deep drinking cup) and a pomegranate (or apple). To the right, a garlanded woman holds a thyrsos (a special staff carried by maenads). In this scene, we are in Dionysos's realm: the three women, one certainly a maenad and the others possibly also, celebrate a festival. One noteworthy aspect of this scene is the seriousness of mood communicated by the set of bodies and heads and by the gestures. On the back, another trio of women display interest in wine: one holds a drinking horn and another a thyrsos, while a third looks on.

This is the name vase of the Chicago Painter. When scholars—particularly J. D. Beazley of Oxford University—set about identifying the hands of the individual artists who had been active in Attic vase painting of the sixth and fifth centuries B.C., groups of vases were often found, on the basis of technical and stylistic similarity, to be the work of a single artist who had not, however, signed any of his surviving work. So it became necessary to give names to these anonymous artists; and they received names for various reasons. The Chicago Painter is so called because this stamnos, which is the key vase

exemplifying his style and technique, is in the collections of The Art Institute of Chicago. (JGP)

28. Lekythos (Oil Bottle)

This lekythos, or oil bottle, provides a good example of white-ground painting, which came into its own in the High Classical Period (c. 450–400 B.C.). The technique, which relied on outline drawing and black relief lines at first, was used on several larger shapes, such as the krater; but the white ground was fragile, and therefore not suitable for vases that were to be in frequent use. Accordingly, it was used especially on lekythoi, which were often deposited in burials and so were exposed to little handling. This specialized function meant that white-ground lekythoi were often decorated with scenes appropriate to funerary contexts such as tombs themselves, farewell scenes, or visitors to a tomb. Painters were later tempted to try other colors; before the end of the century, red, black, and brown were in use for contours, while washes of green, purple, and blue were sometimes used for broader passages.

Lekythoi were favored gifts for male burials, since they were popular as containers of the oil with which young athletes cleaned themselves. This lekythos is quite typical, showing a farewell scene on the main

Detail of Neck

24. Rhyton (Drinking Vessel) in the Shape of a Donkey Head
Greek (Attic), said to have been found at Nola, Italy
Painted by Douris
c. 460 B.C.
Earthenware, red-figure technique; h. 20 cm (7⅞ in.)
Museum Purchase Fund, 1905.345
References: J. D. Beazley, *Attic Red-Figure Vase-Painters* (Oxford, 1963), p. 445, no. 259; Moon, *Greek Vase-Painting in Midwestern Collections*, pp. 190–91.

25. Kylix (Drinking Cup)

Greek (Attic), close to the style of
the painter Douris
c. 480 B.C.
Inscription: ΗΙΠΠΟΔΑΜΑΣ ΚΑΛΟΣ
(Hippodamas Kalos; "Hippodamas is
handsome")
Earthenware, red-figure technique;
h. 7.3 cm (2⅞ in.)
Gift of Martin A. Ryerson, 1907.323
References: Beazley, *Attic Red-Figure
Vase-Painters,* p. 450, no. 23.

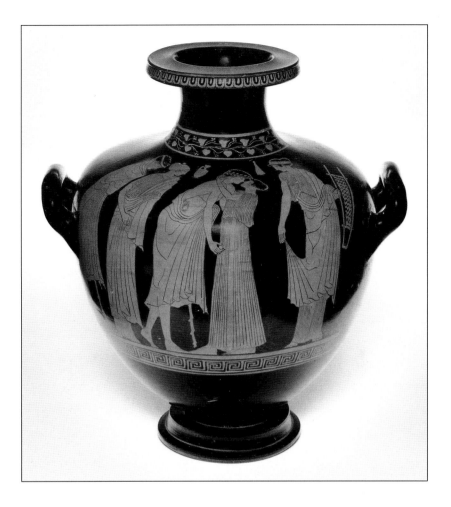

26. **Hydria (Water Jar)**
Greek (Attic), said to have been found
at Nola, Italy
The Leningrad Painter
460/450 B.C.
Earthenware, red-figure technique;
h. 42.4 cm (16¾ in.)
Gift of Martin A. Ryerson, 1911.456
References: Beazley, *Attic Red-Figure
Vase-Painters*, p. 572, no. 88; Moon,
*Greek Vase-Painting in Midwestern
Collections*, pp. 52–53

frieze. The older man (with stick and cloak) salutes the departed youth, a warrior, who holds his spear proudly. Some of the washes of color added to the garment have faded away. This vase has the distinction of having been painted by a leading exponent of red-figure painting, the Achilles Painter (named for his depiction of Achilles on an amphora in the Vatican Museum), who also tried his hand at the white-ground technique. (JGP)

29. Coin Showing a Gorgon

The three Gorgon sisters were winged and bearded daughters of the marine deities Phorkys and Keto, and lived "at Earth's end, near Night," on some islands in the Atlantic—as far west as the Greeks could imagine. Sthenno the Strong and Euryale the Wide Leaper were immortal, but their sister Medusa was not. She was the lover of Poseidon (another marine deity), "he of the black mane," as Hesiod calls him in *Theogony.* By Poseidon, Medusa begot the winged horse Pegasus. Perseus killed Medusa with Athena's help, and got the use of Pegasus while

Athena kept the magical head to put on her aegis as a means of overcoming evil. The god of healing, Asclepius, was said to use Medusa's blood to cure or to kill men.

Why would a Macedonian city want Medusa's head on their coinage? Macedonia, on the northern fringe of the Greek world, was in horse-breeding territory, and Neapolis itself was on the coast. What better protective deity than a marine goddess who specialized in horses? Besides, the same protective virtue of Medusa that appealed to Athena would also be useful to the mercenary soldiers paid with these coins. In later Hellenistic art, Medusa was sometimes portrayed as intensely beautiful, except for her snaky hair; here, her face is comically, almost affectionately fierce, and without the disturbing snakes. (TGD)

30. Statuette of a Seated Girl

The use of terracotta as a medium for the production of sculptural figures goes back to early times, and is trace-

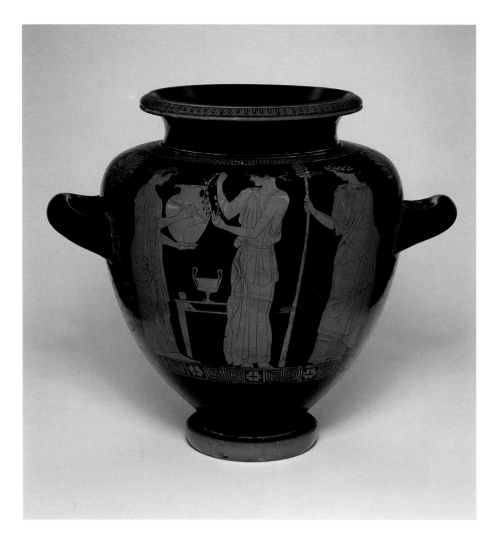

27. Stamnos (Wine Jar)
Greek (Attic), said to have been found
at Capua, Italy, in 1884
Name vase of the Chicago Painter
c. 450 B.C.
Earthenware, red-figure technique;
h. 37 cm (14⅛ in.)
Gift of Philip D. Armour and Charles L.
Hutchinson, 1889.22
References: Beazley, *Attic Red-Figure
Vase-Painters,* p. 628, no. 4; Moon,
*Greek Vase-Painting in Midwestern
Collections,* pp. 197–99.

Detail

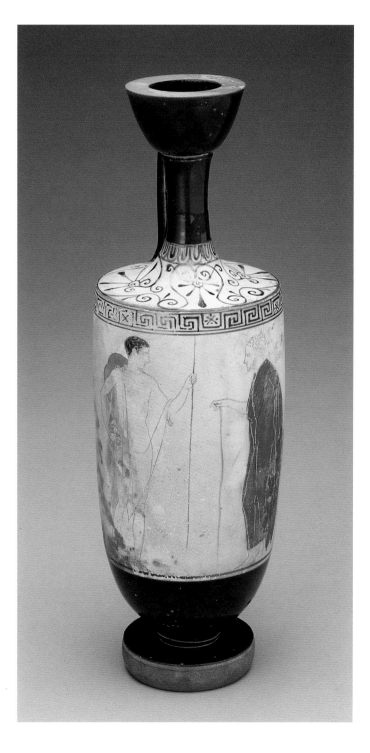

28. Lekythos (Oil Bottle)
Greek (Attic)
The Achilles Painter
450/440 B.C.
Earthenware, white-ground technique;
h. 30.8 cm (12⅛ in.)
Gift of Martin A. Ryerson, 1907.20
References: Beazley, *Attic Red-Figure
Vase-Painters*, p. 1000, no. 199; *Bulletin
of The Art Institute of Chicago* 1, 1
(Oct. 1907), pp. 12–13.

able through the Bronze and Dark Ages to the Geometric, Orientalizing, and Classical periods in Greece. The material, clay, was plentiful and therefore cheap. It was used to create offerings to the gods: images of deities, devotees, or animals that either commemorated athletic success or stood as substitutes for sacrifice. Many of these sculptural figures have been found in sanctuaries, and, because most were mass-produced from molds, hundreds have been discovered.

Children do not appear as a familiar theme in Greek sculpture until the fourth century B.C., when sculpture moved from representing traditional classical types to investigating the world of reality in all its diversity. This shift in representation led sculptors even to the use of caricature and the macabre, and to portray all kinds of emotional states—anguish, pain, brutality, anxiety, pleasure. This interest reached its height in the Hellenistic period (c. 323–31 B.C.). In such a gallery of human types and experience, children played an important role.

The cheerful smiling child here belongs to a type of which several examples have come to light in Attica, most notably in late fourth-century contexts in the sanctuary of Artemis at Brauron. This type is characterized by the child's high-girt chiton, broad round face, and centrally parted hair. This terracotta statuette may have functioned in antiquity as a votive offering in a sanctuary, or as a toy, or perhaps both. (JGP)

31. Funerary Stele (Grave Marker)

Marble relief sculpture was used by the Greeks from the sixth century B.C. to decorate public buildings, most notably temples, with mythological and heroic stories arranged on friezes or in pedimental groups, for votive offerings to the gods, and for grave markers. The most

31. **Funerary Stele (Grave Marker)**
Greek (Attic)
c. 330 B.C.
Marble; h. 152 cm (60 in.)
Alexander White Collection, 1928.162
References: Margarete Bieber, "An Attic
Tombstone in The Art Institute of
Chicago," *Art in America* 30 (1942),
pp. 104–09; Cornelius C. Vermeule,
Greek and Roman Sculpture in America:
Masterpieces in Public Collections in the
United States and Canada (Berkeley,
Calif., 1981), p. 115.

well-known example of architectural sculpture in relief is doubtless the frieze that decorated the Parthenon at Athens. A substantial series of votive reliefs and numerous examples of funerary reliefs have also been found in Athens.

This Attic funerary stele dates to the fourth century, when such stelae were produced in great numbers. The architectural framework has been lost; the three-figure composition is not unusual. The standing male with bowed head and the seated male are stock types; they shake hands in a gesture of farewell that is common enough to be banal. Three-quarter and intermediate views, receding planes, details of folds and tucks of drapery, and the contrast of cloth with flesh are confidently handled by the sculptor. The head of the standing male is entirely in the round. More unusual is the gesture of the female figure, whose right hand is laid flat against the garment over the standing male's left shoulder; this, too, may be a signal of farewell. The irregular bunching of drapery atop her left arm is also rare, while the emotional intensity of her gaze contrasts sharply with the calm detachment of the other two figures. Though badly damaged, this stele is a fine example of Attic sculpture of the middle years of the fourth century B.C. (JGP)

32. **Coin Showing the God Zeus**

The kings of Macedonia had always shown horses on

their coins, and Philip II personalized this tradition by commemorating, on the reverse, his own victory in the horse races of the Olympic Games. The head of Zeus on the obverse of this coin was also a personal touch, since the family of Philip claimed descent from the god. In the years ahead, Philip's son Alexander, who became famous as Alexander the Great, and some of Alexander's successors would exploit this claim as they rose to power (see cat. nos. 11, 12, and 33).

The strong mark Philip left on the coins of his time is a reflection of the tremendous impact Philip was to have on Macedonia, and on the Greek world. Philip expanded the borders of semi-barbarian Macedonia to incorporate the gold mines of the Pangaeus mountain; the resulting wealth funded the professional army and the enlightened despotism of Philip, who encouraged trade, artistic and intellectual contacts with Greece—even engaging Aristotle as private tutor for young Alexander. That the arts flourished under Philip is evident in the superb, naturalistic modeling of both the horse and rider and of the fine head of Zeus on this coin. (TGD)

33. Coin Showing Alexander the Great

After the death of Alexander the Great, his successors scrambled to carve out their spheres of action. Lysimachus, a longtime companion and former bodyguard of Alexander, focused on building a power base in Thrace and extending it to include his native Thessaly. His rare personal courage—he once grappled with a lion—and brilliance as a general were more impressive than his lukewarm gifts as an administrator.

As did all of Alexander's successors, Lysimachus profited from the publicity value of his long association with Alexander. Having usurped the title of king in 306 B.C., Lysimachus began to mint coins of his own (not reissues of Alexander's), yet these coins evoked Alexander far more than the new king. The obverse of this coin bears an idealized portrait of Alexander with the mark of his divinity, the horns of Amun (see cat. no. 12). The reverse is more remarkable, if more subtle. At first glance, this image could almost be taken for the enthroned Zeus holding an eagle, which appeared on the reverse of Alexander's silver coinage. But instead Lysimachus replaced the figures with the Athena and

32. Coin Showing the God Zeus
Reverse: Horseman with victory palm; above, ΦΙΛΙΠΠΟΥ (Philippou; "[minted by] Philip")
Greek (Pella, Macedonia)
359–336 B.C. (reign of Philip II), Pella mint
Silver tetradrachm; diam. 2.6 cm (1 in.)
Gift of Martin A. Ryerson, 1922.4923

33. Coin Showing Alexander the Great
Reverse: Athena enthroned holding Nike (Victory); ΒΑΣΙΛΕΩΣ ΛΥΣΙΜΑΧΟΥ (Basileos Lysimachou; "[minted by] Lysimachus, King")
Greek (Kingdom of Thrace)
306–281 B.C. (reign of Lysimachus of Thrace), Ephesus mint
Silver tetradrachm; diam. 3.1 cm (1¼ in.)
Gift of Martin A. Ryerson, 1922.4924

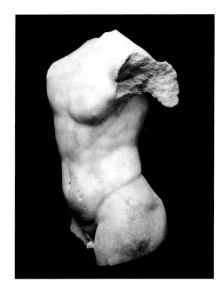

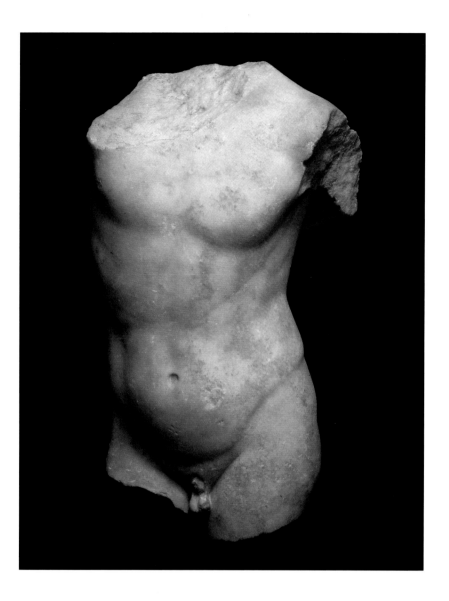

34. Torso of a Youth
Hellenistic or Roman copy of a fourth-
century B.C. Greek original
2nd/1st century B.C.
Marble; h. 66.2 cm (25 ½ in.)
Robert A. Waller Fund, 1926.441

Nike from the two sides of Alexander's gold coinage. Thus, Lysimachus managed to advertise both his valuable connection with the divine Alexander and his own royal autonomy, as the little Nike extends a royal diadem over the words "King Lysimachus." (TGD)

34. Torso of a Youth

The Greeks began to use marble for sculptural figures in the round toward the end of the seventh century B.C. when quarries on the islands of the Cyclades (Naxos and Paros) and on Samos were opened. From the beginning, the standing nude male figure was an important type, and was used during the sixth century in a stiff, abstract style, either as a commemorative grave marker or as an offering to a god in a sanctuary. In the period of transition between the Archaic and Classical periods,

motion and emotion, character, age, and mood were introduced into these figures. Yet, in the High Classical Period (c. 450–400 B.C.), the Argive sculptor Polykleitos attempted to impose mathematically ideal proportions on the type, and to fuse his ideal proportions with the reality of appearance.

The standing nude male figure continued as a dominant type in the fourth century, with renewed interest in movement, expression of mental states, and age. This torso is an adaptation, perhaps from the later Hellenistic or early Imperial era, of a Greek original of the fourth century B.C. The pose of the hips shows that the original statue stood with its weight on the left leg. The thrust of the left hip and the slanting shoulder create a pronounced S curve, often associated with Praxiteles and typical of torsos of the later fourth century. Smooth modeling of

35. Loutrophoros (Water Jar Used as a Funerary Vessel)

Greek, from Apulia, in Italy
The Varrese Painter
c. 365 B.C.
Earthenware, red-figure technique;
h. 88 cm (34¾ in.)
Katherine K. Adler Fund, 1984.9
References: A. D. Trendall and Alexander Cambitoglou, *First Supplement to the Red-Figured Vases of Apulia,* Bulletin Supplement no. 42 (London, 1983), p. 45, pls. IV-1 and 2.

36. Coin Showing Persephone ("Kore")
Obverse: ΚΟΡΑΣ (Koras;
"[coin of] Kore")
Reverse: Nike and trophy; around,
[ΑΓΑΘ]ΟΚΛΕΙΟΣ (Agathokleios; "[coin
of] Agathocles")
Greek (Syracuse, Sicily).
310–307 B.C., issued by Agathokles,
tyrant of Syracuse (reigned 317–289 B.C.)
Silver tetradrachm; diam. 2.7 cm (1 in.)
Gift of Martin A. Ryerson, 1922.4908

the surface and soft forms suggest the youth of the figure. A diagonal swath of drapery across the back perhaps originally ran across either arm and fell down either side, thus framing the figure. (JGP)

35. Loutrophoros (Water Jar Used as a Funerary Vessel)

In the later sixth and fifth centuries B.C., Athens was the center of production of vases painted in the red-figure technique. But in the later fifth and fourth centuries, centers that challenged and ultimately displaced Athens were established in southern Italy and Sicily. Red-figure vase painting continued, however, in Athens until a final flowering, characterized by much added color (yellow, white, gold, blue, and green) in the middle years of the fourth century, after which production stopped around 320 B.C. While the red-figure technique declined in Athens, it prospered in southern Italy in four principal centers of production: in Apulia (the heel of Italy and environs), Lucania (the south-center of Italy), Campania (around Naples), and at Paestum (Poseidonia).

Loutrophoroi were used for ritual cleaning in the ceremonies that preceded a marriage or in funerary rites of the unmarried. This example, perforated through the bottom, served the latter function. On the shoulder, female heads, richly bedecked, appear in agitated floral settings; handles have a serpentine, dynamic shape; vertical zones of palmettes separate the scenes on front and back. At the front, scenes show moments of preparation for a marriage. The bride's entourage displays the needed paraphernalia: mirrors, a fan, jewelry, garlands, oil, and the mystical *cistas* (boxes or caskets with ritual implements). At the back, other female figures carrying gifts visit a tomb. Do these scenes suggest the death of a bride-to-be?

The painter of this jar is known as the Varrese Painter. He was a popular painter with a recognized style char-

acterized by repeated stock figural types. Over 150 vases have been attributed to him. (JGP)

36. Coin Showing Persephone ("Kore")

This exquisite coin owes its design to political violence and ambition. It was minted to commemorate the victory of the would-be king Agathokles over his political rivals in Syracuse and their dangerous Carthaginian allies in 317 B.C. As such, it is the first Sicilian coin to represent the military rather than the agonistic (athletic) aspect of Nike (Victory). On the reverse, Nike is shown, not crowning a young athlete, but nailing captured armor to a trophy. Sicily was wealthy, powerful, and sophisticated; the cosmopolitan city of Syracuse had long prided itself on the high quality of its artists—including its coin engravers—and Agathokles continued that tradition.

The obverse of this coin is less explicitly political than the reverse, but it nonetheless has political overtones. The older coinage of Syracuse had as its obverse type the local spring nymph Arethusa, who was pictured with wavy, water-tousled hair while surrounded by dolphins. By the end of the fourth century B.C., she had become somewhat identified with another maiden goddess, Persephone (Kore). With this coin, the merging of these elements is complete: whereas seaweed once wreathed the nymph's hair, here Kore is crowned with grain in homage to Sicily's fame as the breadbasket of the Mediterranean (Kore's mother/double is Demeter, goddess of grain and all the fruits of the earth). To ensure that the metamorphosis is recognized, Kore's name is spelled out on the coin. It has been suggested that Agathokles, while not wanting to tamper too much with the successful and recognizable coinage of Syracuse, still preferred to abandon the local nymph Arethusa in favor of a pan-Sicilian grain goddess who would advertise the fact that he now ruled nearly the entire, wheat-wealthy island. (TGD)

Etruscan Art

RICHARD DE PUMA

Professor, School of Art and Art History
University of Iowa

The Etruscans are the least familiar of the major classical Mediterranean cultures. Their beginnings may be traced back to about 1000 B.C., but a recognizable Etruscan civilization was not apparent in Italy until around 750 B.C. Later they had major cities throughout west central Italy, and by the fifth century B.C. they had colonized areas to the north (Po Valley region), south (Campania), and west (Elba and parts of Corsica). The zenith of their commercial and military power was reached about 500 B.C. The long and erratic decline that followed did not affect the production or quality of art in most Etruscan cities, some of which peaked culturally in the fourth century B.C. or later. By about 100 B.C., Rome had conquered or absorbed most of the Etruscan cities. Etruscan hegemony in Italy was dead, but their religion, art, and language continued to influence Roman civilization for many years.

Unlike their rival contemporaries, the ancient Greeks, the Etruscans have not bequeathed a complex literary record of their history, religion, and society. This should not imply, however, that they were illiterate. On the contrary, both Greek and Roman writers indicate that the Etruscans had a rich and diverse literature, especially in the areas of religion and divination. Furthermore, many thousands of Etruscan inscriptions do survive, but most, unfortunately, are simple epitaphs giving little information beyond the name and age of the deceased. The relatively few longer documents that survive, while they help scholars to decipher the language, are often frustratingly incom-

plete and generate more questions than answers.

This deficiency in the literary record forces us to rely more heavily on the archaeological record than we do when attempting to reconstruct many other ancient civilizations. Yet, even the Etruscan archaeological record is skewed: almost all of the material remains are from cemeteries, not from domestic or public buildings. Therefore, our ideas of everyday life in ancient Etruria depend excessively on funerary goods rather than habitation sites.

Despite these many limitations, scholars have made much progress in gaining a better understanding of Etruscan culture. One cannot underestimate the appeal that their intriguing art has for most modern viewers. Even a cursory investigation of Etruscan artistic production reveals that they did much more than simply attempt to copy Greek art. No one can deny that Greek art had a strong impact on Etruscan artists, and there is growing evidence that a number of Greek artists worked in Etruria. But as more material is discovered, we see much that is highly distinctive and thoroughly original in Etruscan art. The Greeks, who rarely lavished praise on the work of "barbarians," certainly recognized their talents for they comment on the Etruscans' superior skills in metalworking. Likewise, the archaeological record corroborates their judgment: thousands of bronze objects show considerable aesthetic and technical sophistication, and Etruscan gold jewelry is arguably the most innovative and magnificent of the classical world.

Although the Art Institute's collection of Etruscan art is small, many of the pieces are of high quality. Some can be used to illustrate differences between Greek and Etruscan art. In the case of the bucchero kyathos (cat.

FACING PAGE: *Hand Mirror*, 470/450 B.C.
(detail of cat. no. 37).

no. 39), for example, one finds a typically Etruscan shape produced and decorated in a distinctively Etruscan technique; there is, frankly, nothing Greek about this object. The bronze mirror (cat. no. 37) shows the vibrant complexity of the artistic situation in ancient Etruria. While this type of object certainly existed in ancient Greece, Greek mirrors are infrequently decorated with engraved scenes. The Etruscans, on the other hand, seem to have produced many more mirrors (more than 3,500 are known today), and most of them are engraved with complicated figural scenes. The subject matter may have been adapted from Greek mythology, but the treatment, both iconographically and stylistically, is almost always distinctly Etruscan. The Etruscan love of terracotta also comes through in the Art Institute's female votive head (cat. no. 40) and architectural relief (cat. no. 38). Unlike the mainland Greeks, who rarely used terracotta for large sculptures or temple ornament, the Etruscans produced over life-sized terracottas for the decoration of their temples.

Despite their often fragmentary nature, many works of Etruscan art retain an aura that evokes pleasure and astonishment from modern viewers. A careful examination of a work of Etruscan art is never unrewarding.

ITALY

ETRURIA

Vulci

Tiber River

CORSICA

Tarquinia

Rome

Cerveteri

Praeneste

Veii

LATINUM

ADRIATIC SEA

Neapolis

Tarentum

CAMPANIA

SARDINIA

SICILY

MEDITERRANEAN SEA

Carthage

Syracuse

$\mathcal{E}$*arly Italy*

37. Hand Mirror

The mirror was cast of solid bronze and then polished. The obverse, or original reflecting side, is decorated with a series of volutes engraved just above the tang, an extension that once held a now missing handle of bone or ivory. The reverse, or non-reflecting side, is elaborately engraved with a scene that depicts the death of the hero Memnon. According to Greek legends, Memnon was the son of Eos, goddess of the dawn, and Tithonos, brother of King Priam of Troy. The king of Ethiopia and an ally of the Trojans in their war against the Greeks, Memnon was killed by Achilles, another product of a divine mother (Thetis) and a mortal father (Peleus).

The mirror shows Eos (whom the Etruscans called Thesan) holding the body of her dead son. She stands on an elegant ground line below which is engraved a pair of volutes. Ivy frames the entire scene. Eos wears voluminous drapery and has intricately engraved wings. Her nude son drops his helmet and sword.

The popularity of this particular subject on Etrus-can mirrors at this time may be due to the fact that many women, the owners of these objects, had lost sons in a series of wars. They may have found solace in knowing that even a goddess had suffered an identical loss. The workshop that made this mirror was probably located in the ancient city of Vulci, a major center of bronze production. (RD)

38. Architectural Relief Showing a Gigantomachy

Despite its fragmentary nature, this dramatic terracotta relief preserves a good deal of its original coloring. Three headless figures engage in violent combat. At the center is a muscular, winged male whose legs terminate in snakelike coils. Behind him on the left is a large male who wears drapery over his left shoulder but whose chest is exposed. To the right is a striding female figure dressed in a *chiton,* a long sleeveless garment with an apronlike overfold. Both males are painted with a brown ocher to portray their tanned bodies. Pink and light blue pigments decorate the wing feathers on the central male;

37. **Hand Mirror**
Etruscan, probably from Vulci
470/450 B.C.
Bronze; h. 16.9 cm (6⅝ in.)
Katherine K. Adler Fund, 1984.1341
References: Richard De Puma, *Corpus Speculorum Etruscorum, U.S.A. 1: Midwestern Collections* (Ames, Iowa, 1987), p. 60, no. 41, figs. a-e.

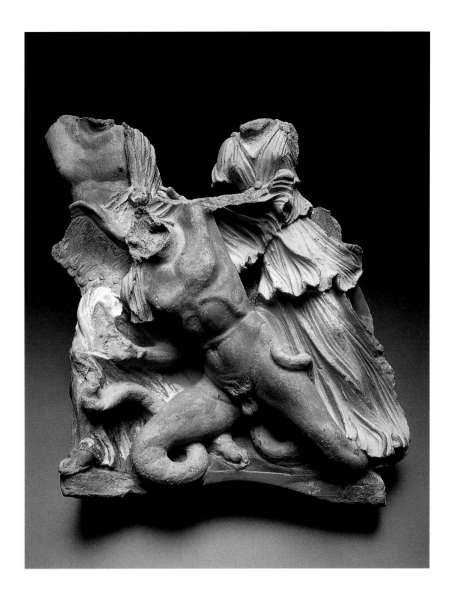

**38. Architectural Relief Showing
a Gigantomachy**
Etruscan
3rd/2nd century B.C.
Terracotta and pigment; h. 45.8 cm
(18 1/16 in.)
Katherine K. Adler Fund, 1984.2
References: Maria José Strazzula, "Motivi
Pergameni in Etruria a Proposito di una
Terracotta Architettonica con Giganto-
machia a Chicago," *Archeologia Classica*
43 (1991).

his serpent legs are stippled with black paint and small tool marks to add texture.

The subject of this small sculpture is clearly a gigantomachy, or battle of gods and giants, a frequent subject in both Greek and Etruscan art. The style and composition of this terracotta are strongly influenced by Hellenistic treatments of the subject, especially the famous second-century altar of Zeus and Athena at Pergamon, in Turkey, which is known for the exaggerated musculature, violent movement, and intense pathos of its relief sculpture.

The gigantomachy in the Art Institute's collection once decorated an Etruscan building, probably a small temple. This fragment was most likely one of a series of similar compositions that functioned as antefixes, the ornamental covers that protect the lowest row of tiles on a roof. (RD)

39. Stemmed Kyathos (Drinking Cup)

The tall foot and bowl of this single-handled vase or kyathos, were thrown on the potter's wheel. Its large handle, however, was constructed by hand and attached to the bowl before firing. The vase is decorated with a series of applied ridges on both the pedestal foot and the exterior of the bowl; in addition, there are modeled protuberances near the points where the handle is attached to the bowl's rim and a round buttonlike ornament at the top of the handle. Incised decoration, executed before firing, consists of horizontal rows of zigzags at the base of the foot and around the exterior of the bowl. The most elaborate incisions appear on the inner face of the handle, including more zigzags and two plantlike forms of vertical lines from which emanate three pairs of volutes. If any of these incisions have symbolic meaning, it is now lost.

This kyathos is an excellent example of bucchero, a characteristic type of Etruscan black pottery produced in great quantities from the seventh century B.C. onward.

The kyathos shape in terracotta no doubt derives from metal prototypes, as is apparent in the rotelles on the handle that imitate the fastening elements on bronze vessels but have no practical function in clay. Many bucchero kyathoi of this particular type have been found at or near the ancient city of Vulci, and it is likely that they were made there throughout the second half of the sixth century B.C. (RD)

40. Votive Head

This molded terracotta depicts the head of young woman who wears a diadem, now fragmentary, over a veil. The facial features are distinctly modeled and stylized. She has almond-shaped eyes, sharply-defined, arched eyebrows, and pursed lips shown in the "archaic smile." Her flaring ears are pierced with large holes, no doubt for the addition of metal earrings. Her hair is rendered in an abstract pattern of wavy vertical locks. Vestiges of reddish pigment on the hair, the right pupil, and the back of the head suggest that the terracotta was originally painted.

Terracottas of this sort, depicting the heads of generic young men and women, are a common feature of Etruscan votive production. The Etruscans, like the Greeks and Romans, frequently dedicated small sculptures of heads, body parts, children, divine groups, and animals to various protective deities at their temples and shrines.

Detail of Neck

39. **Stemmed Kyathos (Drinking Cup)**
Etruscan, possibly from Vulci
550/525 B.C.
Earthenware, bucchero ware; h. 42 cm
(16⅛ in.)
Gift of Edward H. Weiss, 1980.620

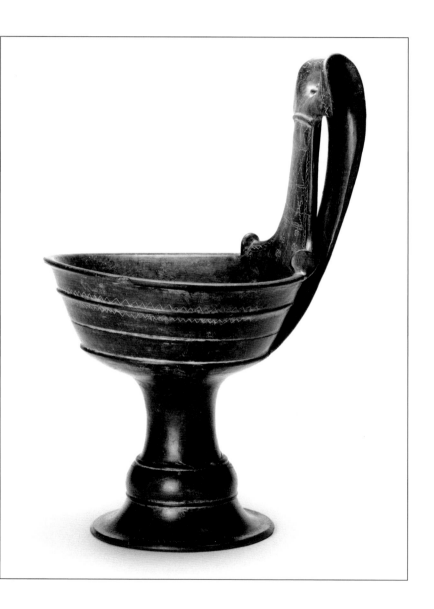

40. **Votive Head**
Etruscan, possibly from Veii
c. 500 B.C.
Molded terracotta and traces of pigment;
h. 26.5 cm (10½ in.)
Katherine K. Adler Fund, 1975.342
References: Louise Berge and Warren G.
Moon, "An Etruscan Votive Head in the
Classical Collection," *Bulletin of The Art
Institute of Chicago* 72, 1 (Jan.-Feb.
1978), pp. 2–5; Steven George Smithers,
"The Typology and Iconography of
Etruscan Terracotta Curotrophic Votives:
The Heads and Bambini" (Ph.D. diss.,
University of Iowa, 1988), pp. 61–63, 67,
69, 96, 266, and 291–92 (cat. no. 22).

These votive offerings were intended to help win the favor or assistance of the deity in some special effort, or to thank the deity for benefits already received. Large quantities of votives have often been found buried in pits near a temple or cult site.

The type represented by the Art Institute's head was clearly derived from Attic *korai,* or maiden figures, sculpted in Athens around 530–500 B.C. The closest Etruscan parallels come from the so-called Campetti votive deposit at the ancient city of Veii, just north of Rome. It is likely that the Art Institute's terracotta head was made in southern Etruria, perhaps at Veii itself. (RD)

Roman Art

CORNELIUS C. VERMEULE III

Curator of Classical Art
Museum of Fine Arts, Boston

In the year 31 B.C., the young Octavian defeated his Roman rival Mark Antony and Queen Cleopatra of Egypt in a sea battle off Western Greece. With Antony's and Cleopatra's suicides at Alexandria in Egypt, Octavian became ruler of the Roman world. Named Augustus in 27 B.C. by the Roman Senate, he was recognized as the first Roman emperor. His world, and that of his successors, extended from the British Isles to the Tigris River, the area of modern Iraq. The Romans were soldiers, builders, and merchants. They knew what they liked in art, but they were first to admit that their Greek citizens and subjects could create the sculptures and jewelry that Romans desired and could buy.

Roman art is a story of Roman taste. The Romans loved portraits of themselves. They embellished their public spaces with statues and busts of their emperors, like Hadrian (reigned A.D. 117–38), who loved Greek art and traveled the Empire at the height of its prosperity. The coins of ancient Rome feature very factual, precise portraits of the famous leaders of the last decades of the Republic and of the emperors on one side (the obverse), and divinities, historical events such as visits to the provinces, famous buildings from temples to aqueducts, and even exotic animals imported to Rome for the games and circuses on the second side (the reverse). Because the coins give the emperors' full titles and offices, we can often date new issues of coins to the month in which they appeared.

Roman respect for the Greek past led to the prodigious copying of famous Greek statues and reliefs made centuries earlier by popular Greek sculptors. This mechanical copying, usually in marble from plaster casts, was done in workshops all over the Roman Empire in order that many Roman cities and the country villas of the rich could exhibit masterpieces otherwise only seen in dimly lit shrines in Greece and Asia Minor. The famous Greek statues were usually in bronze, but many were melted down in the barbarian onslaughts of the Middle Ages. The marble copies that have survived in ruins, however, give us visual insight into lost works of art celebrated by ancient writers. Without these copies, often carved by talented craftsmen who respected the originals, great sculptors of the fifth and fourth centuries B.C., notably Phidias, Praxiteles, Skopas, and Lysippos, would not be understood as fully as they are today.

In the decorative arts, the Romans adapted Greek designs to their terracotta architectural panels, their bronze mirrors, their jewelry, and, above all, their sarcophagi (coffins). Indeed, carved marble funerary chests gave the Romans a marvelous opportunity to narrate Greek myths and heroic scenes such as episodes from the Trojan Wars. The mighty hunter Meleager was popular as a statue identified with Skopas, but his deeds could be told in full on the four sides of a large marble sarcophagus. As the Roman world passed toward the Middle Ages, especially after Constantine the Great's edict of religious toleration in A.D. 315, biblical subjects came to dominate the arts where once the Olympian divinities, the mythological heroes, and the imperial Romans had held the stage.

FACING PAGE: *Statue of Meleager*, c. 50 B.C. (detail of cat. no. 41).

GAUL

DACIA

SPAIN

Nîmes
Grauferesque • • *Arles*

CORSICA

ITALY

Tivoli
•Rome

Neapolis
Boscoreale
Herculaneum • *Pompeii*

Mt. Vesuvius

GREECE

• Calydon

Athen.

SICILY

Carthage •

Syracuse

*T*he Roman Empire

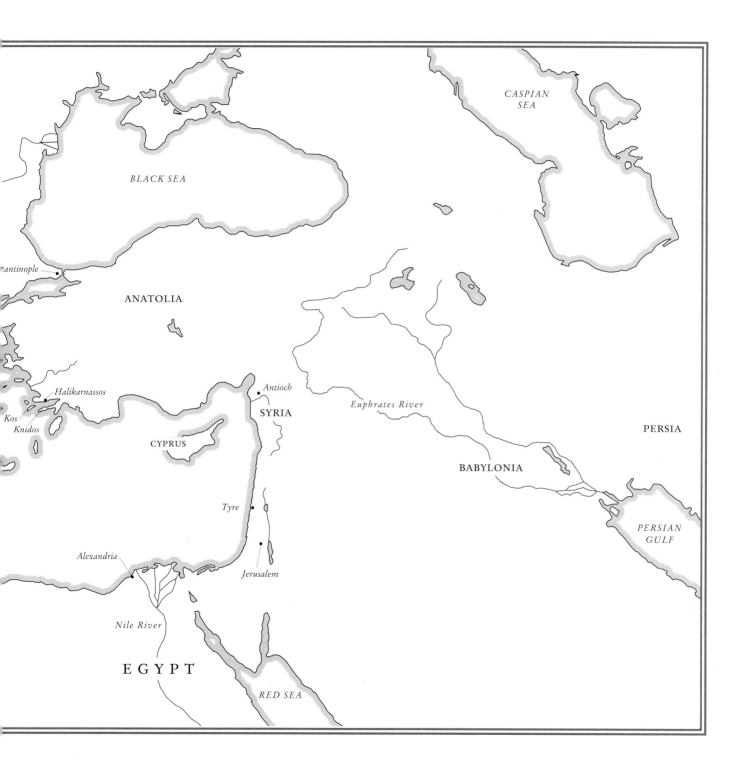

CASPIAN
SEA

BLACK SEA

...antinople

ANATOLIA

Halikarnassos

Kos

Knidos

CYPRUS

Antioch

SYRIA

Euphrates River

PERSIA

BABYLONIA

Tyre

Jerusalem

Alexandria

Nile River

PERSIAN
GULF

EGYPT

RED SEA

41. Statue of Meleager
Roman copy of a fourth-century B.C.
Greek original attributed to Skopas
c. 50 B.C.
Marble; h. 173 cm (68 ⁵⁄₁₆ in.)
Gift of Mr. and Mrs. Eugene A. Davidson,
1972.935
References: Steven Lattimore, "Meleager:
New Replicas, Old Problems," *Opuscula
Romana* 9, 18 (1973), pp. 158 and 166;
Vermeule, *Greek and Roman Sculpture
in America,* p. 21.

42. Coin Showing Consul Marcellus
Obverse: around, MARCELLINVS and
triskeles
Reverse: Consul Marcellus consecrating
trophy; MARCELLVS/COS QVINQ
Roman Republic
50 B.C. (Claudia gens), Rome mint
Silver denarius; diam. 1.9 cm (¾ in.)
Gift of Martin A. Ryerson, 1922.4846A

41. Statue of Meleager

Meleager was a young hunter who led a band of men and his beloved Atalanta against a great wild boar that was ravaging the countryside of Calydon. Meleager killed the beast, but a quarrel over the spoils ensued and the youthful hero killed his mother's brothers. His mother, Althaea, proceeded to engineer her son's death by burning a branch that had been his means to immortality.

This statue is an impressive, early copy of an original attributed to the sculptor Skopas that belongs to the decade before the middle of the fourth century B.C. The original was probably made in hollow-cast bronze, meaning the ungainly tree trunk seen here would not have been necessary to support the statue. On the other hand, the pediment was in marble, and some copies of this Meleager in marble manage this stance without such a large tree. In the original version of the statue, Meleager was leaning on his spear, and the head of the slain boar was on a tree stump near his left leg. The cloak thrown over the left arm adds a touch of restlessness to the composition. Indeed, restlessness in repose was a characteristic of the work of Skopas, who was one of the first sculptors to superimpose emotion on the timeless ideal of Greek representations of young gods, heroes, and athletes. The emotional roller coaster of Meleager's career was the perfect vehicle for Skopas, whether as a caster in bronze or a carver in marble. (CCV)

42. Coin Showing Consul Marcellus

According to legend, Romulus defeated an enemy commander in hand-to-hand combat; to celebrate this event, he built a temple to Jupiter and dedicated to the god the spoils of the battle. It became customary for any Roman general who emulated Romulus to dedicate similarly the resulting special trophy (*spolia opima,* "spoils of honor"). The triumph of Marcus Claudius Marcellus over the Gaul Viridomarus in 222 B.C. is one of the earliest known of such single-handed victories, and his proud descendant Marcellinus commemorated this milestone on the coinage for which he was responsible. Marcellinus also took this occasion to boast of his ancestor's five consulates (thus the inscription "COS QVINQ," literally "consul for the fifth time," on the coin's reverse) and his capture of Syracuse (the triskeles on the obverse).

It is noteworthy that the superb, "realistic" portrait on the obverse is of the stern old republican Marcellus, not his politically ambitious scion. The detailed, naturalistic "likeness" is therefore wholly imaginary, the subject of the portrait being nearly two centuries in the tomb. Roman republican law and custom forbade the representation of any living person on its coinage. It was not until Julius Caesar evoked long-dormant royalist thoughts among some of his supporters that the Senate bestowed this telling privilege on the oft-appointed dictator, shortly after this coin was minted. Others followed suit: Pompey the Great, Octavian, even the tyrannicide Brutus left us their own portraits; and no subsequent ruler, regent, or would-be usurper of Rome failed to have his or her visage immortalized on a coin. (TGD)

43. Architectural Relief Panel

The Romans of the early Empire loved to decorate the wooden moldings or plaster walls of their houses and villas, such as those at Pompeii and Herculaneum, with relief panels fired to the color red from high-grade clay.

43. **Architectural Relief Panel**
Roman, said to have been found in Italy
in the 19th century
1st century A.D.
Molded terracotta; h. 58.8 cm (23¼ in.)
Katherine K. Adler Fund; restricted gift
of Mr. and Mrs. Kenneth Bro, the Classical
Art Society, and Mr. and Mrs. Walter
Alexander, 1990.87

Scenes such as the one shown here were prepared with a mold that could be used to repeat the same composition as a frieze extending the length of the wall or alternating with related subjects from different molds. The designs were often in an older style, from the rich heritage of the Greek past. Such is the case with the rare scene presented here. Two female temple-attendants, servants of a goddess such as Artemis, are kneeling with an elaborate altar between them. The altar takes the form of a tall candlestick (or candelabrum) with offerings burning on the top and a stand with large floral scrolls at the bottom. The costumes of the attendants, as well as their hairstyles, are designed to recall the Greeks of southern Italy (at Locri under the toe of Italy) and Sicily (at Catania just across the Straits of Messina) in the period around 200 B.C. The egg-and-dart molding above and the interlaced waterleaves below provided a continuum with the panels on either side of this one, panels in which the main decoration may have been different, modeled from other molds. The four nail-holes in the background were for tacking this panel to its architectural setting. (CCV)

44. Statuette of an Enthroned Figure

Seated on her elaborate, high-backed throne, this goddess or personified virtue wears a long chiton tied above her waist and an ample himation, which is draped over her left shoulder, falls down her back, around her lap, and ends in folds across either side of her legs. Her right hand is extended, palm upwards. Her missing left arm was raised. A cap culminating in a large diadem is set above her hair, the latter tied in a long braid behind her shoulders. The Romans placed small statues such as this in their household shrines. Depending on details of cos-

44. Statuette of an Enthroned Figure
Roman
1st century A.D.
Bronze, with eyes inlaid in silver;
h. 15.5 cm (6⅛ in.)
Wirt D. Walker Fund, 1965.402

45. Bracelet
Roman, probably
from Italy
1st/2nd century A.D.
Gold; l. 22.3 cm (8⅞ in.)
RX18051.1

46. **Statuette of Hercules**
Roman copy of the fourth-century B.C.
Greek original by Lysippos
2nd century A.D.
Bronze; h. 22 cm (8¹¹⁄₁₆ in.)
Katherine K. Adler Fund, 1978.308

tume and the attributes in each hand, they could represent major divinities such as Juno and Ceres or personifications such as Fortuna, Pietas, or Concordia. Because this impressive figure probably held a *patera* (libation dish) on her right hand and a large cornucopia (horn of plenty) in her left arm, she is probably Concordia, symbol of family harmony and one of the four cardinal virtues of the Roman Empire. In A.D. 15, the second Roman emperor, Tiberius (reigned A.D. 14–37), dedicated a large temple to Concordia just below the Capitoline Hill and overlooking the Roman Forum, the most important location in the Roman world. This bronze is a version in miniature of the colossal gold and ivory cult-image of Concordia placed in that temple and now known chiefly from Roman coins. (CCV)

45. Bracelet

The Romans loved heavy, showy, and complex jewelry. While the Aphrodite of Knidos might wear one bracelet on her left upper arm, the small marble and bronze

Aphrodites found in the houses of Pompeii and Herculaneum are very much in keeping with Roman taste, which might favor vulgar, heavy bracelets on both upper and lower arms and similar, elaborate objects around the ankles. Nothing could be more Roman than a bracelet formed of golden hemispheres, almost like grapes, set with and set off by rosettes and with complex links and clasps. Touches of granulation hint at the Etruscan or native Italic traditions which lie behind Roman jewelry. This bracelet could have been found in the ruins of Pompeii or Herculanuem, for there are similar ensembles in the museums of Italy and elsewhere in Europe from the cities overwhelmed by the lava and pumice of Vesuvius on that fateful August day in the year A.D. 79. An identical bracelet in the National Museum at Naples does indeed come from Pompeii. The taste for such jewelry, bracelets, and necklaces, was carried to the eastern end of the Mediterranean in the second century A.D. and, eventually, along the caravan and shipping routes to the Indian subcontinent and beyond to the Far East. (CCV)

46. Statuette of Hercules

This small bronze statue of superior workmanship and in excellent condition gives us a splendid insight into the appearance of a lost masterpiece in bronze by Lysippos, a famous sculptor working around 335 B.C. Lysippos made many statues in bronze, and a favorite theme, which he probably portrayed more than once during his long career, was the weary Herakles (the Roman Hercules). The hero is shown resting from his Twelve Labors while holding the three golden apples of the Hesperides against his lower back with his right hand. With his left hand he grasps a club for support. The skin of the Nemean lion is often shown wrapped around this arm or hanging from the club. The most famous version of this statue was probably made by Lysippos for the Gymnasium of his native city of Sikyon, along the Gulf of Corinth, on the northern coast of the Peloponnesus. This small bronze shows a wreath of vine leaves and fruit (grapes?) around the forehead, suggesting the pleasures of the banquet that await the hero on completion of his labors. This may be a Roman Imperial addition to the hero's attributes. On sarcophagi and in mosaics of the decades from A.D. 150 to 230, the drinking contest between Dionysos (the Roman Bacchus, god of wine) and Herakles was a popular theme, for it pitted experience and toleration against rashness and force. The weary Herakles always succumbed in these encounters and had to stagger off to bed with the aid of Dionysos's followers, the satyrs and maenads. (CCV)

47. Portrait Head of the Emperor Hadrian

Of all the Roman emperors, Hadrian (reigned A.D. 117–38) is the one whose portrait is most frequently found, all over the Empire from Britain to Persia, from Asia Minor to Egypt. The grateful Greek cities dedicated 125 statues to Hadrian around the precinct of the Temple of the Olympian Zeus at Athens, a colossal structure that Hadrian (honored there as the Thirteenth Olympian, or god of Mount Olympus) paid to have completed. And, among all his portraits, few are the equal of this likeness in conveying the complex, neurotic character of the emperor who inherited the Roman world at its greatest extent from his fellow Spaniard Trajan (reigned 98–117) and who consolidated the Empire by backing away from the military quicksands of Mesopotamia and the mountains beyond in Parthia or Persia (modern Iran). Hadrian spent much of his reign traveling from city to city, from outpost to oasis. Hadrian was also the first emperor to grow a beard; it is said that he grew it to conceal a scar from a hunting accident and to resemble the Greek philosophers whom he respected. Most of his successors continued the fashion until Constantine the Great (reigned 306–37), who modeled his appearance on Helios (god of the sun) and on Christ. Hadrian's memory was so cherished in the East and West in the Middle Ages that both the Roman and Orthodox churches have a saint named Hadrian or Adriano(s). (CCV)

47. Portrait Head of the Emperor Hadrian
Roman
2nd century A.D.
Marble; h. 36 cm (14¼ in.)
Katherine K. Adler Fund, 1979.350
References: Vermeule, *Greek and Roman Sculpture in America*, p. 309.

48. Relief of a Fallen Warrior from the Shield of the Athena Parthenos

Around 435 B.C., the sculptor Phidias enriched the front of the shield at the side of his gold and ivory Athena in the Parthenon with scenes of Greeks and Amazons battling in the Trojan Wars, or, perhaps more likely, fighting around the Athenian Acropolis in the kingship of Theseus. In Roman times, certain figures from this complex struggle were lifted out of context and enlarged to

49. Statue of a Seated Woman
Roman copy of a fifth-century B.C.
Greek original in the style of the
Parthenon sculptures
2nd century A.D.
Marble; h. 82 cm (32⅜ in.)
Katherine K. Adler Fund, 1986.1060
References: Louise Berge, "'A Lady
Seated on a Rock. . .' Now in The Art
Institute of Chicago," *The Ancient World*
15 (1987), p. 50, nos. 3 and 4.

**48. Relief of a Fallen
Warrior from the Shield of the
Athena Parthenos**
Roman copy of the fifth-century B.C.
Greek original by Phidias, found in the
harbor of Piraeus
2nd century A.D.
Marble; h. 48.1 cm (19 in.)
Gift of Alfred E. Hamill, 1928.257
References: A. D. Fraser, "The
'Capaneus' Reliefs of the Villa Albani
and The Art Institute of Chicago,"
American Journal of Archaeology 43
(1939), p. 449, fig. 2; Vermeule, *Greek
and Roman Sculpture in America,* pp. 21
and 44, fig. 18, pl. 4; Helen Comstock,
"Five Centuries of Greek Sculpture,"
International Studio 84 (June 1926), pp.
33–35 (ill.); D. von Bothmer, *Amazons in
Greek Art* (Oxford, 1957), pp. 209–14,
pl. 87.

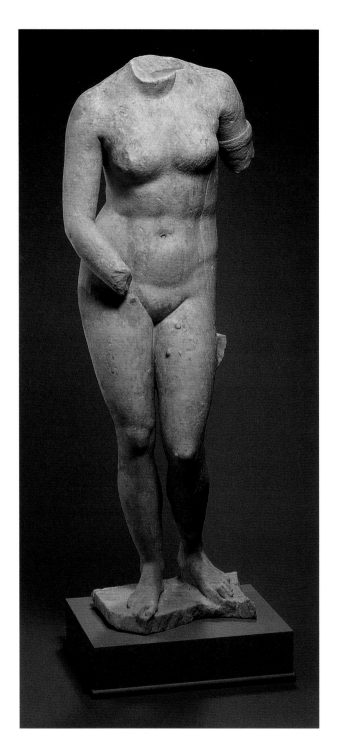

become decorative relief-panels for the walls of a colonnade or courtyard. When this relief was first discovered, this figure of a wounded Greek sinking to the ground with cloak and shield was misnamed "Kapaneus" after one of the Seven Heroes who died trying to capture the city of Thebes in Greece in mythological times. The dying warrior's noble countenance, the fillet or ribbon tied around his forehead, and the figure's powerful, athletic body sum up what Phidias and his pupils sought to project as the ideal of mature male dignity in the decade when Athens was at the height of its power in the eastern Mediterranean world. This Phidian style, translated from a circular golden shield to a rectangular marble relief, was exactly what collectors such as the emperor Hadrian sought to decorate their palaces and villas. Athenian sculptors of the Roman Empire made a good living creating and exporting such memories of past glories. This relief and a number of others were found in Piraeus Harbor, where they had been lost in some disaster while awaiting shipment. (ccv)

49. Statue of a Seated Woman

Throughout the Roman Imperial Period, the sculptures of Athens in the Golden Age of chief magistrate Perikles and his master sculptor Pheidias impressed institutions and citizens all over the ancient world, especially around Rome and the Bay of Naples. The seated, draped goddesses in the pediments of the Parthenon on the Acropolis were adapted for use as individual statues of divinities and of empresses or other notable women. In this statue, the heavy, crinkled folds of drapery in the long undergarment tied with a rope at the waist and the heavy cloak hanging from the left shoulder and thrown across the lap have been made the salient characteristics of a heavy figure full of dignity. The head, neck, and forearms were carved separately and attached with cement and dowels. Since the figure sits on a large rock rather than a throne, a goddess seems to have been intended, perhaps a major deity such as Hera (known in ancient Rome as Juno), who was the consort of Zeus (the Roman Jupiter), the ruler of the divinities who lived on Mount Olympus in northern Greece. There is, however, the strong possibility that this statue commemorated a Roman empress or even that it was intended as a memorial statue of a private citizen of renown. An empress such as Faustina the Elder, wife of Antoninus Pius, who was made a goddess and equated with Juno after her death in A.D. 141, or her daughter Faustina II, wife of Marcus Aurelius, who was accorded similar status by the Roman Senate in 175, seem likely candidates for the subject of this statue. (ccv)

50. **Statue of the Aphrodite of Knidos**
Roman copy of the fourth-century B.C.
Greek original by Praxiteles
2nd century A.D.
Marble; h. 168 cm (66⅙ in.)
Katherine K. Adler, Harold L. Stuart,
and Wirt D. Walker funds, 1981.11

51. Portrait Head of a Young Woman
Roman, said to have been found in
Athens
2nd century A.D.
Marble; h. 22.5 cm (8⅞ in.)
Edward A. Ayer Fund, 1960.64
References: Cornelius C. Vermeule, "Two
Masterpieces of Athenian Sculpture," *The
Art Institute of Chicago Quarterly* 54, 4
(Dec. 1960), pp. 8–10; Cornelius C.
Vermeule, *Roman Imperial Art in Greece
and Asia Minor* (Cambridge, Mass., 1968),
pp. 364–65, fig. 179; George M. A.
Hanfmann, *Roman Art* (New York,
1975), no. 98; Helga von Heintze, "Ein
spätantikes Mädchenporträt in Bonn: Zur
stilistischen Entwicklung des Frauen-
bildnisses im 4. und 5. Jahrhundert,"
Jahrbuch für Antike und Christentum 14
(1971), p. 78, no. 4, and pp. 80–81, pl. 13d
and 15a; Kurt Weitzman, ed., *Age of
Spirituality: Late Antique and Early
Christian Art, Third to Seventh Century,*
exh. cat. (New York, 1979), pp. 289-90,
no. 268; Evelyn B. Harrison, "The
Constantinian Portrait," *Dumbarton
Oaks Papers* 21 (1967), pp. 87–89, fig. 31;
Vermeule, *Greek and Roman Sculpture in
America,* pp. 372–73.

52. Hand Mirror
Roman
2nd century A.D.
Gilded bronze; diam. 11.8 cm (4¹¹/₁₆ in.)
Gift of Mr. and Mrs. James W. Alsdorf,
1985.1042
References: W. Hornbostel, *Aus Gräbern
und Heiligtümern* (Mainz, 1980),
pp. 271–73 (ill.).

50. Statue of the Aphrodite of Knidos

Around the middle of the fourth century B.C., working in his studio in the shadow of the Athenian Acropolis, Praxiteles made a statue of Aphrodite fully clothed and, daringly for his times, a second statue of the goddess emerging from her bath and wearing only a bracelet on her upper arm. Praxiteles offered the choice of his two marble sculptures to the city of Kos on the island of the same name. Beset with modesty, the good burghers bought the draped statue, which was promptly forgotten by the later peoples of the ancient world. The city of Knidos, on a peninsula of Asia Minor not far southeast of Kos, bought the nude Aphrodite, and both statue and city enjoyed great fame ever after. So popular was the Knidian Aphrodite that many copies were made in later times and sold everywhere. The statue seen here is one of them. Bereft of head, hands, and draped *kalpis* (water jug) by her left leg, it is hard to appreciate the rhythmic composition of the original statue. With the surfaces of the marble so weathered and worn, it is hard to grasp the soft, translucent beauty of the Knidia, as this Aphrodite was called. At Knidos, the original sculpture stood in a circular Doric tempietto, the small building open to the sky. Hadrian so admired the ensemble that he had the little temple and the statue copied for a knoll near the modern entrance to his villa at Tivoli. It seems very likely that the Art Institute's copy was placed in a similar setting, in an area where the climate was not kind to the statue. (CCV)

51. Portrait Head of a Young Woman

This elegant young lady with her hair wrapped in braids around her head to form a kind of turban is something of an enigma. Did she live around A.D. 140 or did she belong to the early years of Constantine the Great, around 315 when these hairstyles were revived? Lovers of Roman portraiture have been split down the middle on this question over the past thirty-five years. Whenever she lived and sat for her portrait—and the better guess is around 140—she summed up all that was forthright as well as elegant in Roman portraiture. The white marble of the face has been given a cameo-like polish, something just becoming fashionable in portrait sculpture after 130, and the carving and incising of the pupils of her eyes give her a lifelike intellect that reflects the highest quality in Roman portraiture. (CCV)

52. Hand Mirror

Artemis (the Roman Diana), or a Roman lady with divine fantasies, after her bath in a rustic, woodland setting, is the subject of the tondo in relief on the back of this Roman hand mirror. Her cloak is draped over the rocks on which she sits, and she holds the end wrapped around a small hand mirror in her raised left hand, a divine celebration of the uses of the mirror in a Roman household. The landscape in front of her, to the right, recalls the paintings and reliefs from houses around the Bay of Naples before the eruption of Mount Vesuvius in A.D. 79. The quiver of the goddess leans against the base of a garlanded altar with a small herm on top. A second terminal figure, Priapos, the god of gardens and fertility, tilts back while facing to the right on the ledge at the right. The bovine skull in the right foreground suggests the sacrifice after a successful hunt. The spreading tree in the background is a device to unite the whole composition. As a result of these details and artistic devices, the composition as a whole is both elegant and precise, with a touch of the erotic in the details that befits the vanities and personal qualities of just such a domestic work of art. (CCV)

53. Coin Showing Empress Julia Domna

Obverse: around, IVLIA AVGVSTA ("Augusta" means "Revered" or "Venerable")
Reverse: "Piety" offers incense at altar; around, PIETAS AVGG (Pietas Augustorum; "Proper attitude among the imperial family")
Roman Empire
c. A.D. 199–207, Rome mint
Gold aureus; diam. 2 cm (¾ in.)
Gift of Martin A. Ryerson, 1922.4883

53. Coin Showing Empress Julia Domna

Julia Domna is usually referred to either as the wife of the Emperor Septimius Severus or as the mother of Caracalla and Geta. This coin, in fact, was issued during the joint reign of Severus and his elder son, but by their authority, not her own. Yet Julia was no mere relative to power; as the self-assured portrait on this coin suggests, her influence was openly recognized by contemporaries. Intellectual, ambitious, and steel-willed, the Syrian-born Julia was called "the philosopher" and was famous for her circle of learned friends; at the same time, she could successfully vie with courtiers to influence imperial policy, and could accommodate herself to Caracalla's murder of her younger son Geta. The empress Julia would remain a guiding force in Caracalla's reign, taking her own life after his assassination in A.D. 217.

The figure of Piety on the reverse is a standard type, invoking the traditional Roman attitude of respect and duty toward one's family, country, and gods. As such, it would appear a singularly inappropriate choice of values to grace a coin of the ruthless Severan dynasty. But the suspicious death of Severus, the near-breakup of the Empire, and the murder of Geta were, at the time of this minting, still in the future; and Julia "Augusta" might well have hoped that her strong presence might maintain proper *pietas* (respect) among the august members of her family. (TGD)

54. Head of Mars

In about 345 B.C., a sculptor named Leochares, who later worked in Athens, was commissioned to fashion a colossal, standing statue of Ares (the Roman Mars) for the god's Temple at Halikarnassos on the peninsula just east of Kos and north of Knidos. The god was portrayed, wearing a helmet and a cuirass, and holding his shield and his spear. The city of Halikarnassos was somewhat isolated in terms of the main centers of the Greek and Roman world, but its tomb of King Mosollus, a vast ensemble of sculpture and architecture on which Leochares had worked, was one of the Seven Wonders of the Ancient World, giving its very name (mausoleum) to an elaborate tomb anywhere in any age. The Mausoleum of Halikarnassos brought touring Roman magistrates and generals to the city. Admiration for the statue of Ares in the temple overlooking the city and for the very military qualities of the Mausoleum of Helikarnassos led to free copies of these works being made for shrines elsewhere. This head captures the grandeur of the original statue, and at the same time includes something of the softness of form for which such fourth-century sculptors as Praxiteles became

54. Head of Mars
Roman
2nd century A.D.
Marble; h. 59.2 cm (23⅓ in.)
Katherine K. Adler Fund, 1984.1
References: Louise Berge, "A War God in Chicago," *The Ancient World* 10, 3–4 (1984), p. 66.

famous. These qualities were later reflected in the work of copyists and adapters in Roman times. (CCV)

55. Fragment of a Sarcophagus

This fragment or secondary section of a large sarcophagus, made in Athens around the years A.D. 240 to 250 and exported to the eastern Mediterranean, appears to show the heroes grouped around Meleager at the time of the hunt for the Calydonian boar. Atalanta sits at the right, and Herakles is seated with his club at the left.

Meleager, standing with his foot on a rock between two other companions, has been made to resemble the heroic or divine Macedonian king, Alexander the Great. Perhaps this is because the scene on the sarcophagus was based on a painting of the period around 300 to 200 B.C. in which Meleager's hunt and tragic death were equated with Alexander the Great's conquests and his own untimely demise at Babylon in 323 B.C. Alexander was a great hunter as well as a great general, and his life ended by decree of the Fates, the same three sisters who had doomed Meleager to die by hitching his thread of life to a firebrand. The reliefs of sarcophagi were fraught with the symbolism of death and tragedy, since they were bought by grief-stricken relatives as well as patrons of the arts. This poetic presentation of the young hunter Meleager amid other young heroes whose features resemble those of the companions of Alexander the Great stands in contrast to the solid statue of Meleager identified with Skopas in the years before the middle of the fourth century B.C. (see cat. no. 41). (CCV)

56. Coin Showing Emperor Caracalla

Caracalla was only ten years old when his father Septimius Severus granted him the title of co-Augustus and Pontifex (priest) and bestowed on him the Tribunitian power. The young emperor, however, aged quickly. This portrait shows a sixteen-year-old who knows he will soon control most of the civilized world. By all accounts a mild and charming youth, Caracalla's nature was corrupted by power—or else power allowed his true nature to reveal itself. The coin portraits of this emperor chronicle, year by year, the toll that time and Empire took on Caracalla's once pleasant and boyish face. It is a horrific and fascinating spectacle; not least remarkable is that the engravers were allowed to portray the cruelty and debauchery reflected in the emperor's visage in the later coinage. In this coin portrait, the attempts against his father's life, the murder of his younger brother Geta, the massacres of Roman citizens, and the brutality of the circus games were still in the future, masked by the dis-

55. Fragment of a Sarcophagus
Roman, said to have been found near Antioch, Syria, probably made in Athens
A.D. 240/250
Marble; 96 cm (37⁷⁄₁₆ in.)
Gift of the Alsdorf Foundation, 1983.584
References: Guntram Koch, "Zu einem Relief in der Alsdorf Collection," *Archäologischer Anzeiger* (Berlin, 1978), pp. 116–35; Cornelius C. Vermeule, "Dated Monuments of Hellenistic and Graeco-Roman Popular Art in Asia Minor: Pontus through Mysia," in *Studies Presented to George M. A. Hanfmann* (Cambridge, Mass., 1971), p. 176 (old no. 57.1968); Vermeule, *Greek and Roman Sculpture in America,* p. 246 (old no. 57.1968); Cornelius C. Vermeule, in *The Search for Alexander,* (Boston, 1980), p. 119, no. 40.

arming, somewhat enigmatic smile of the youthful emperor.

The figure of Victory and the title on the reverse refer to the successful campaigns against the Parthians, waged by Severus, in which Caracalla took part, despite his tender years. His real name was Marcus Aurelius Antoninus; he received his nickname for affecting to wear a Gaulish cape called a "caracalla." (TGD)

57. Coin Showing Emperor Constantine the Great

Constantine's coinage is as complex as the age that produced it. The Empire was undergoing radical changes, among them the short-lived experiment in shared government called the Tetrarchy, in which pairs of senior and junior emperors were to divide the burden of running the sprawling and unruly Empire. Self-effacing cooperative spirit was not, however, a highly developed concept among aspiring emperors, and by A.D. 313 Constantine the Great emerged as sole ruler. In order to concen-

trate his energies where the chances of Roman greatness remained the strongest, Constantine moved the seat of the government to the Thracian city of Byzantium, engaged on an ambitious building program, and renamed the "New Rome" in honor of himself: Constantinople.

The portrait of Constantine on the obverse of this coin is among the last in the history of Roman coinage, for increasingly the emphasis lay not on the individual person of the emperor but on the office. Luxurious robes and diadems, elaborate court ceremony and a nearly mystic atmosphere of awe surrounded the emperor, and transformed the human ruler into a quasi-divine being in the eyes of the ruled: true portraiture gave way to symbolic representations. Constantine's luminous eyes in this coin portrait were said by his contemporaries to reflect his divine inspiration, whether that inspiration ultimately came from Sol or from the Christian God, to whose religion Constantine officially converted the Empire, though his grasp of the underlying concepts remains doubtful. (TGD)

Ancient Glass

KURT T. LUCKNER
Curator of Ancient Art
The Toledo Museum of Art

Colorful, malleable, transparent—the qualities of glass are wondrously varied, even magical. Its fluidity and endless chromatic possibilities have been admired for millennia. Yet glass is difficult and dangerous to manipulate. The extreme heat required to fuse the basic components into the glowing red-hot molten glass that issues from the glass furnace prevents glassmakers from ever touching their work directly. Only after laborious effort and after a work of glass has been finally removed from an annealing kiln can the true result of the glassmaker's art be seen. It is no wonder that, during its early history, glassmaking was practiced by only a few craftsmen. Their works were treasured like gold and were commissioned by kings to enhance the ambience of wealth and power of their courts.

Around 2300 B.C., the secret of glassmaking was discovered somewhere in the Near East. There the use of vitreous glazes on fired tiles, ceramic vessels, and beads had reached a high level of sophistication, as had experiments with faience, a glasslike material made by fusing powdered quartz or sand. These technologies probably led to the discovery of glassmaking, which requires furnace heat to fuse the three ingredients of glass: sand (silicon dioxide), alkali oxide (such as soda ash or natron), and lime. All of these materials were inexpensive and readily available, but the method of combining them seems not to have been widely known or practiced.

The earliest known glass objects are all opaque and brilliantly colored. Many of the colors seem to reproduce the appearance of semiprecious colored stones prized in the Bronze Age—the blues of lapis lazuli and turquoise and the reds of carnelian and jasper. Thus, glass was first treasured because of its ability to mimic other more valuable materials. It is therefore understandable that early glass was worked when cold using the same techniques—cutting, grinding, and polishing—as the rare stones it resembled.

From the time of its discovery, glass continued to be used in the ancient Near East for small, fine objects such as beads, inlays, and cylinder seals. It was not until about 1500 B.C. that glass vessels were made, probably in northern Mesopotamia. Because the earliest glass vessels have been found only at sites known to have been dominated by the Hurrian kingdom known as Mitanni, the people of Mitanni have been credited with making the first glass vessels.

Mesopotamian Core-Formed Glass, 1600–1200 B.C.

Virtually all Near Eastern vessels were made by the core-forming technique (see cat. no.58), a laborious and exacting process that remained the principal technique for making glass vessels for over 1500 years. The consistent shapes (derived from contemporary Mesopotamian ceramic vessels) and decoration (colorful glass threads tooled into festoons, zigzags, meanders, and eyes) suggest that, from the late sixteenth to the thirteenth century B.C., glass vessels were produced by only a few

FACING PAGE: *Fragments of Roman Mosaic Glass,* 1st century B.C./1st century A.D., Gifts of Theodore W. and Frances S. Robinson, Henry H. Getty, and Charles L. Hutchinson.

glassmaking centers in close contact with each other. Their products, commissioned and controlled by powerful patrons, have been found almost exclusively in temple ruins, palaces, and lavishly furnished graves.

Egyptian Core-Formed Glass, 1550–1200 B.C.

In Egypt, the beginnings of glass vessel making are well documented. Egypt's dry climate has preserved perfectly a multitude of vessels brought to light by numerous excavations. Only a few Egyptian glass objects predating the New Kingdom have been found, but the production of glass vessels for scented oils and unguents appears suddenly as a mature industry under the pharaohs of the Eighteenth Dynasty (1550–1307 B.C.). The earliest Egyptian glass vessels come from tombs dating to the reign of Tuthmosis III (1504–1450 B.C.). During the Eighteenth and Nineteenth Dynasties, the working of glass was restricted to a handful of workshops producing vessels and objects only for the pharaoh and his court. The glass inlays amid gold, silver, calcite, and faience decorations on the pharaoh Tutankhamen's throne attest to the esteem in which the Egyptians held glass.

Eastern Mediterranean Core-Formed Glass, 900 B.C.–A.D. 10

With the collapse of the wealthy Bronze Age civilizations in Mesopotamia, Egypt, and Greece, glassmaking seems to have virtually stopped for about 300 years until the ninth century B.C., when it reappeared in Syria, Mesopotamia, and Egypt. By the late seventh century B.C., all of the major glassworking techniques had been revived throughout the eastern Mediterranean. Most common among these was the core-forming technique used, as before, to make small sealable vessels to hold scented oils and unguents. These eastern Mediterranean core-formed vessels differ from their courtly Bronze Age predecessors. Glass was now a normal, though perhaps costly, commodity of daily life, used by ordinary people, as witnessed by the appearance of glass vessels in scenes painted on contemporary Greek vases.

Hellenistic Glass, 323–30 B.C.

After Alexander the Great's conquest of the Near East, his court and the kingdoms of his successors demanded luxury items. The fabulous wealth of the Hellenistic period created a demand not only for objects of gold, silver, ivory, and bronze, but also for more novel luxuries that the medium of glass could provide. Molded, engraved, and cast mosaic wares of endless colors and patterns appeared now in larger, open shapes for use as tableware. The use of glass for tableware rather than just for small precious vessels indicates the increasing demands of a wealthy clientele.

Roman Glass, 50 B.C.–A.D. 100

With the rise of Rome as an international power, luxurious Hellenistic glass vessels were transformed into vessels to suit Roman taste. Expensive cast and engraved luxury glasses were still produced, but new glassmaking processes sprang from the impetus of the Hellenistic traditions. The Art Institute's handsome cast ribbed bowl (see cat. no. 61) typifies these new Roman wares. While ribbed bowls were important as the first mass-produced Roman tableware, they also marked the end of casting as a major glassmaking technique in the ancient world.

Roman Free-Blown Glass, 40 B.C.–A.D. 650

Around 40 B.C., at a time when glass technology was

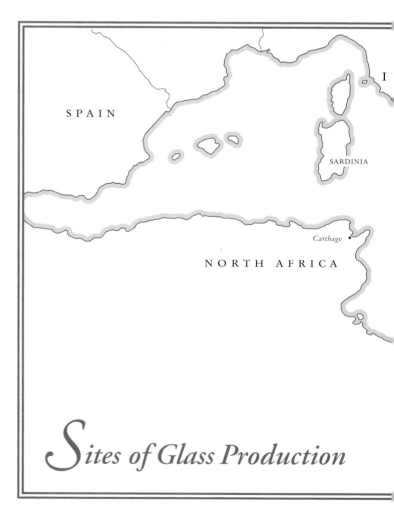

*S*ites of Glass Production

making unprecedented strides, the greatest single discovery since the invention of glassmaking itself occurred: glass could be inflated. Glassblowing must have developed from experiments in picking up heated pieces of cullet (raw chunks of glass) on the end of a long, hollow tube through which the glassmaker could force his breath. It was quickly realized that through repeated reheatings in the furnace and the use of tools, the inflated bubble of glass could be quickly and cheaply fashioned into vessels of any shape and size. But by the middle of the first century A.D., glassblowing had become the principal means of forming glass vessels. Greater quantities of glass vessels than ever before flooded the market, and glass became virtually commonplace in Roman life.

Roman Mold-Blown Glass, A.D. 25–650

Within a century after the invention of glassblowing, the technique of blowing glass into reusable molds was discovered, probably in the vicinity of Sidon on the Syrian coast (now Lebanon). Glass vessels could now be shaped and decorated in a single step. Thousands of vessels were produced inexpensively and quickly from a single clay or metal mold, which could be easily replaced or fitted with new sections as needed through a sequence of generations. The mold-blowing process continues to be used to this day.

With the end of the Roman Empire in the West, and the shift of its capital to Constantinople in the East in the fourth century, glassmaking centers in the eastern Mediterranean continued Roman glassmaking traditions. The collection of ancient glass at The Art Institute of Chicago includes many significant types from twenty-three centuries of glassmaking in the ancient Mediterranean world. The selection of glass vessels included here, which ranges from the courts of Egypt's warrior pharaohs to the shrines of Byzantine Jerusalem, documents the strengths of this important collection.

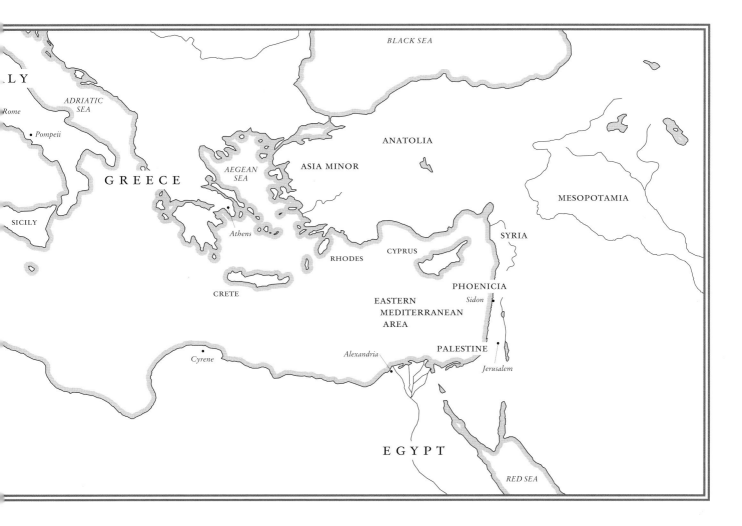

58. Kohl Container in the Shape of a Palm Column

Egyptian
New Kingdom, late Dynasty 18 or 19,
1400–1225 B.C.
Rod-formed glass with applied rim-disk
and thread decoration; h. 8.9 cm (3½ in.)
Gift of Theodore W. and Frances S.
Robinson, 1941.1084
References: Geraldine J. Casper, *Glass
Paperweights in The Art Institute of
Chicago* (Chicago, 1991), p. 9 (ill.).

58. Kohl Container in the Shape of a Palm Column

Glassworking in Egypt appeared suddenly as a fully developed industry during the reign of the pharaoh Tuthmosis III, and was most probably imported from the older glass centers of Palestine and Syria. In addition to small glass objects such as beads, amulets, and inlays, the new industry also produced a wide variety of glass vessels for unguents, incense, and cosmetics.

Particularly popular were vessels like this example made to contain kohl, a black pigment used by both men and women to outline their eyes. The kohl was applied with a thin rod, and the vessels were sealed with stoppers made of linen and wax. The shape of this vessel recalls a palm column, a traditional element of Egyptian architecture and also a shape already well established

for kohl containers in a variety of other materials.

The bright, opaque colors of these early core-formed glass vessels—dark blue, turquoise blue, red, yellow, and white—seem to emulate intentionally semiprecious stones such as lapis lazuli, turquoise, and jasper. The rarity of these glass vessels (only some five hundred complete ones are known) and the fact that most of them have been discovered in tombs and the ruins of glass workshops serving the royal palaces at Thebes, Malkata, Lisht, and Tel el-Amarna indicate that they were a precious commodity made by an elite corps of craftsmen for members of the royal court. The costly technique of core forming established at this time continued to be the primary process for making glass vessels for the next fifteen centuries. (KTL)

59. Unguent Bottles of the Sixth to Fourth Centuries b.c.

Beginning in the late thirteenth century B.C., the great Bronze Age civilizations that had flourished in the Near East, the eastern Mediterranean, and Egypt came under attack and either collapsed or fell into marked decline. Palace workshops producing luxury goods, particularly glass objects and vessels for royal and noble patrons, virtually disappeared. It was not until the ninth century B.C. that the glassmaking techniques of the Bronze Age reappeared. The core-forming technique, which had reached such a high level of perfection under Egypt's pharaohs of the Eighteenth Dynasty, now reemerged as the preeminent glassworking technique, but not in Egypt. Although no glass workshops have been discovered, Rhodes, southern Italy, the Syro-Palestinian coast, and Cyprus have all been suggested as probable areas of manufacture.

The new core-formed vessels were used for the same purposes as their Bronze Age prototypes—as containers for valuable scented oils, unguents, and cosmetics. Unlike their ancestors found in royal tombs and palaces, however, these vessels have been found in domestic settings where they held cosmetics, in sanctuaries where they were placed as votive offerings, or in graves where empty glass vessels were placed after their contents had been used to anoint the deceased. The core-forming technique and the colors used to make these vessels are identical to those of Egyptian glass vessels (see cat. no. 58). It is notable that the body color of all of these vessels—dark blue mimicking prized lapis lazuli—continued the most popular body color of Eighteenth Dynasty glasses. (KTL)

60. Unguent Bottles of the Fourth to First Centuries B.C.

The vessels represented in this group have been discovered principally in Italy, with a modest number found around the Aegean, leading to suggestions that the most important centers of glassworking had shifted to Italy and perhaps Macedonia during the third century B.C. Although far fewer core-formed vessels were produced in this period (about one-quarter the number known from the late sixth to the mid-fourth century B.C.), the array of shapes and variations on them increased significantly from twenty to thirty-six. The Art Institute's hydriske and footed lentoid aryballos illustrated here, which are among the newly introduced shapes, are unusual and rare examples of their kind.

Later in the Hellenistic period, from about 200 B.C. to about A.D. 10, glass workshops on the Syrian coast and on Cyprus abandoned most of the refined vessel shapes of the fourth and third centuries B.C. in favor of

only two—the alabastron and the amphoriskos (see illustration). The tall-necked amphoriskos, with its long handles and base-knob, imitates the common Hellenistic amphorae used to transport wine around the Mediterranean world. The pale green transparent glass handles of this group are significant, for they mark the first use of nearly colorless, transparent glass in the core-forming technique. This pale glass would become standard in the Roman glass industry to follow. (KTL)

61. Ribbed Bowl

Under Roman rule, the luxury wares produced by Hellenistic glass centers were soon supplanted by new glass forms, both containers and tableware, entirely of Roman invention. These wares were produced in great quantities by newly developed casting techniques in an increased number of workshops in both the eastern Mediterranean and Italy itself. Mass-produced glass vessels now filled marketplaces throughout the Roman Empire. For the first time in the ancient world, affordable glass vessels became available to a broad clientele and competed with both ceramics and metalware. Glassmaking had become a true industry.

Typical of early Roman tableware is this handsome monochrome ribbed bowl. The evenly spaced ribs radiating around the lower portion of the bowl were made by an ingenious two-step process whereby the ribs were probably formed by pressing a tool against a heated, cast disk-shaped blank of glass. Next, the disk with its radiating ribs was sagged over a convex form in a furnace to create the bowl's shape. After annealing, the inside of the rim, its upper edge, and the outside of the rim were polished on a lathe. The remainder of the outside, that is the area of the ribs, was fire-polished by direct exposure to the flames in the furnace.

The pale green or pale bluish-green color of these bowls occurs naturally, as the result of iron and other oxides in the sand, one of the essential components used in making the batch of glass. This so-called natural glass became commonplace in Roman glass for centuries to come. (KTL)

62. Unguent Bottle: Alabastron

The political stability of Alexander the Great's empire and that of the several Hellenistic kingdoms established after his death created an international demand for goods, especially luxury goods. Traditional craft industries, particularly glassmaking, flourished from the late fourth to the late first century B.C. While the centuries-old technique of core-forming glass continued, dramatic new techniques were invented by which monochrome and

59. **Unguent Bottles of the Sixth to Fourth Centuries B.C.**
Left to right: Alabastron, Aryballos, Alabastron, Oinochoe, and Amphoriskos
Eastern Mediterranean
Core-formed glass with applied rim-disks, handles, and bases; max. h. 13.9 cm (5½ in.)
Left to right: Gifts of Theodore W. and Frances S. Robinson, 1941.1091, 1941.1083, 1942.637, and 1942.635; Gift of Ebenezer Buckingham, 1891.29

60. **Unguent Bottles of the Fourth to First Centuries** B.C.
Left to right: Hydriske, Lentoid
Aryballos, Oinochoe, Alabastron, and
Amphoriskos
Eastern Mediterranean
Core-formed glass with applied
rim-disks, handles, and bases; max.
h. 14.9 cm (5⅞ in.)
Left to right: Gifts of Theodore W. and
Frances S. Robinson, 1942.628, 1942.629,
1942.632, 1949.1181, and 1942.651

mosaic glass tableware and containers of unprecedented luxury were produced. One particularly lavish group of vessels stands out. These vessels of a variety of shapes are covered with a wavy pattern of narrow bands of sumptuous gold juxtaposed with bands of deep purples, blues, greens, and golden browns.

The technique used to create this unguent bottle was demanding, labor-intensive, and complex. Three thin layers of glass were fused to form the colored cane lengths—a layer of white or yellow between outer layers of translucent, rich color. The gold canes were formed by sandwiching gold foil between layers of colorless glass. These canes were then softened, manipulated, and shaped around a core or rod to form the alabastron.

Gold-band mosaic alabastra like the Art Institute's example were sealed by tall, colored glass stoppers, which also functioned as applicators. These stoppers were hollow tubes open at both ends, topped by a flat disk. When in place, the stopper could function as a sprinkler. A small quantity of the vessel's precious contents could also be removed by placing one's finger over the opening in the disk at the top of the stopper, thereby trapping a little of the liquid in its hollow interior. (KTL)

63. Bowl

The first century B.C. saw the last Hellenistic kingdoms in the eastern Mediterranean fall to Roman expansion. Although a period of such upheaval might have halted the production of the luxury items that had enriched these courts, the opposite is true. Not only did the established

glassworking techniques continue, but exciting new ways of decorating with intricate patterns, which were invented by glass workshops of the Hellenized East, flourished and expanded under Roman rule.

Notable among these new glass vessels is a group recovered in 1900 from a shipwreck that probably occurred around 80 B.C. off the southwest coast of Greece near Antikythera. Among the many items found in the shipwreck were several luxury glass vessels. Five are mosaic glass bowls similar in shape to this one: hemispherical bowls with an upright or slightly outsplayed rim on a stalwart, flaring foot. The discovery of similar examples in Syria, Crete, Greece, and southern Italy has led to the theory that these distinctive bowls were made in the eastern Mediterranean. The Art Institute's footed bowl is a rare example of this Antikythera group, as first noticed in 1986 by David F. Grose. The gauze-like appearance of this bowl is a marvel of glass technology, one of the greatest treasures of the Art Institute's collection of ancient glass. (KTL)

64. Mold-Blown Vessels

Expanding trade throughout the empire and the increased power and wealth of Rome itself attracted luxury industries to Italy with the lure of profit and prominence. It is therefore no surprise that the new technology of mold-blowing glass invented in Sidon soon appeared on the Italian peninsula. Historians are still debating whether the mold-blown vessels discovered on the Italian peninsula were made by Sidonian glass artists who had moved

61. **Ribbed Bowl**
Roman, from the Syro-Palestinian region or Italy
Late 1st century B.C./mid-1st century A.D.
Sagged glass, rotary-polished and fire-polished; h. 4.6 cm (1⅞ in.)
Gift of Theodore W. and Frances S. Robinson, 1949.433

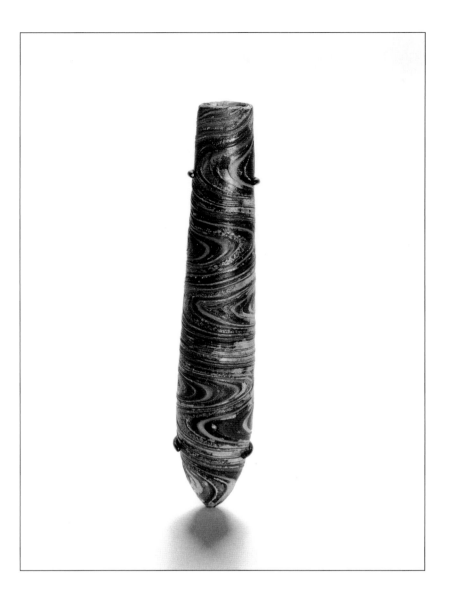

62. Unguent Bottle: Alabastron
Eastern Mediterranean, 1st century B.C.
Probably formed around a rod from
lengths of cane and cast glass, rotary-
polished; h. 14 cm (5½ in.)
Gift of Theodore W. and Frances S.
Robinson, 1941.1099

to Italy or by others copying their molds or designs. By the middle of the first century A.D., the mold-blowing glass industry was well established throughout the empire.

Mold-blowing glass workshops of the Syro-Palestinian coast were particularly well known for their monochrome novelty containers and bottles like those shown here in colors ranging from purple, green, and blue to opaque white. A group of these early mold-blown bottles is decorated with carefully modeled images such as vessels framed in architectural settings, floral sprays, and bowls of fruit. Others were made in the shape of specific fruits or nuts, like this date-shaped bottle. While there are no published analyses of the contents of these bottles, their constricted necks and small mouths sug-

gest that they once held costly scented oils like other small, exotic glass vessels from the earliest period of glass vessel making. Expensive scents have a tradition of being marketed in unusual containers, and for the Romans this seems to also have been the standard practice. (KTL)

65. Jug

The advantages of glass in everyday life must have astounded the average Roman. Unlike vessels made of clay, glass could be easily cleaned and was impervious to liquids like oil or wine stored or shipped in it. Transparency, however, must have been the most novel feature of blown-glass vessels. The nature and amount of a com-

63. **Bowl**
Roman, probably made in Italy, said to
have been found in Hamāh, Syria
Early 1st century B.C.
Cast network mosaic glass with applied
foot; h. 5 cm (2 in.)
Gift of Mr. and Mrs. Theodore W.
Robinson, 1947.888
References: Casper, *Glass Paperweights in
The Art Institute of Chicago*, p. 10 (ill.);
David F. Grose, *Early Ancient Glass*
(New York, 1989), p. 196 n. 51.Mold-
blown glass with applied handle and
tooled rim; h. 15 cm (5⅞ in.)
Gift of Theodore W. and Frances S.
Robinson, 1949.958

modity transported, shipped, and marketed in glass vessels could now be easily verified. Still-life painters were
fascinated by the opportunity to show fruit and wine
through the walls of glass bowls and ewers. In fact,
blown-glass vessels replaced many traditional ceramic
containers within one generation.

From the beginning, blown-glass tableware like this
jug were used on a daily basis in Roman dining rooms
and pantries. A perfect expression of Roman taste, its
decoration does not impede its usefulness. This deep
brown jug could have been made at any point during a
two-hundred-year period. Its elegant, yet eminently
functional shape assured its continued popularity. The
generous loop and the thumb rest above are perfectly
scaled to the human hand. The applied handle and the
vertical trail below, with its rhythmic repetitions of
crimped peaks, give the vessel a measured amount of aesthetic interest without impeding the its use. Vessels like
this became a mainstay of Roman life, and factories serving the everyday market flourished throughout the
empire. (KTL)

66. Kohl Container with Elaborate Handle

Among the great variety of glass vessels produced in the
Roman province of Palestine, fancy containers for kohl
were a particular specialty from about A.D. 350 to 625
(see entry on cat. no. 58). Among the numerous types of
these containers, the ones produced during the late sixth

and early seventh centuries are particularly elaborate
and fanciful.

During the sixth century, Palestinian glass workers
began to make taller kohl containers as fashion must
have demanded. By the early seventh century, these vessels had become elaborate confections with looped handles and intricately worked side decoration of looped
trails, like this example. The crossed elements of the
handle tiers, which in fact inhibit the use of the vessel,
and the looped side ribs allowed the glass craftsman the
opportunity for whimsical concoctions, and also provided much-needed structural reinforcement as these
vessels became taller and taller.

Elaborate vessels like this, made late in a continu-
ous three-hundred-year production period, have been
found principally in the inland area of northern
Palestine near the Sea of Galilee. There, the descendents
of the original Jewish inhabitants of this area continued
the long tradition of using kohl and making these glass
vessels. Their workshops vied with each other to pro-
duce more and more elaborately decorated kohl containers. The rivalry led to outlandish creations in which
decoration defeated function. (KTL)

67. Hexagonal Jug with Christian Symbols

Despite the collapse of the Roman Empire in the West
during the fifth and sixth centuries A.D., Roman life in the
eastern Mediterranean continued essentially unchanged.

64. Mold-Blown Vessels
Left to right: Amphoriskos, Hexagonal
Bottle, Cylindrical Jug, and Date-Shaped
Bottle
Roman, from the Eastern Mediterranean
Early 1st century/early 2nd century A.D.
Mold-blown glass, some with applied
handles; max. h. 10.7 cm (4¼ in.)
Left to right: Gifts of Theodore W. and
Frances S. Robinson, 1949.1173,
1943.1171, and 1943.1174; Gift of
G. G. Kohlsaat, 1891.32

65. **Jug**
Roman
Late 1st/early 3rd century A.D.
Blown glass with applied and tooled
handle; h. 13.9 cm (5½ in.)
Gift of Theodore W. and Frances S.
Robinson, 1949.1132

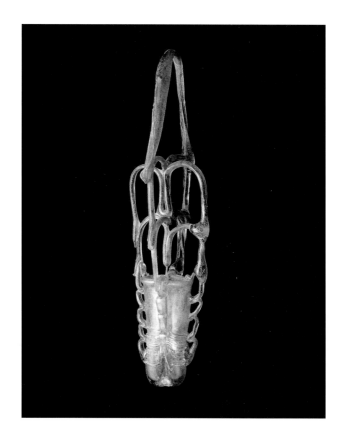

66. **Kohl Container with Elaborate
Handle**
Roman, from Palestine
Late 6th/early 7th century A.D.
Blown glass with applied handle and
thread decoration; h. 32.2 cm
(12⅛ in.)
Gift of Theodore W. and Frances S.
Robinson, 1949.425

67. **Hexagonal Jug with Christian Symbols**
Roman, from Palestine, made in
the vicinity of Jerusalem
A.D. 578/636
Mold-blown glass with applied handle
and tooled rim; h. 15 cm (5⅞ in.)
Gift of Theodore W. and Frances S.
Robinson, 1949.958

From their new capital in Constantinople, Roman emperors ruled the eastern empire, called the Byzantine Empire, until Syria, Palestine, Egypt, and North Africa were conquered by the armies of Islam in the seventh century.

Workshops in the eastern empire continued the traditional Roman glassworking techniques. Among their products, a notable group of mold-blown hexagonal vessels was made for pilgrims in the vicinity of Jerusalem. One workshop in the vicinity of Jerusalem, identified by Dan Barag (see "Suggestions for Further Reading," p. 93), specialized in mold-blown vessels for both Jewish and Christian pilgrims visiting the holy city. The Art Institute's jug, like those of this group made for the Christian clientele, most probably held holy oils from the Church of the Holy Sepulcher.

Three of the six rectangular panels forming the body of this jug show a cross. These crosses have been identified as representing one or more aspects of a monumental cross erected in the second half of the fourth century (or later) on the rock of Golgotha, the site of Jesus's crucifixion. The panel depicting the step and base under the cross (shown here on the right) is particularly important, for it provides evidence for the date of these vessels. Writings of pilgrims visiting Jerusalem in the sixth century mention steps leading to the cross that stood on Golgotha until the Church of the Holy Sepulcher was destroyed by Sasanian invaders in 614. (KTL)

Suggestions for Further Reading

EGYPTIAN ART

Aldred, Cyril. *Akhenaten and Nefertiti*, exh. cat. Brooklyn, N.Y., 1973.

_____. *Egyptian Art.* New York, 1980.

Bothmer, Bernard V., comp. *Egyptian Sculpture of the Late Period, 700 b.c.–a.d. 100,* exh. cat. Brooklyn, N.Y., 1960.

Bourriau, Janine. *Pharaohs and Mortals: Egyptian Art in the Middle Kingdom.* Cambridge, 1988.

The Brooklyn Museum. *Cleopatra: The Age of the Ptolemies,* exh. cat. Brooklyn, N.Y., 1988.

Hayes, William. *The Scepter of Egypt.* 2 vols. New York, 1959.

Iversen, Erik. *Canon and Proportion in Egyptian Art.* London, 1955.

Peck, William H. *Egyptian Drawing.* New York, 1978.

Quirke, Stephen, and Jeffrey Spencer, eds. *The British Museum Book of Ancient Egypt.* London, 1992.

Robins, Gay. *Egyptian Painting and Relief.* Aylesbury, 1986.

Schäfer, Heinrich. *Principles of Egyptian Art.* Oxford, 1980.

Spanel, Donald. *Through Ancient Eyes: Egyptian Portraiture,* exh. cat. Birmingham, 1988.

Wilkinson, Richard. *Reading Egyptian Art: A Hieroglyphic Guide to Ancient Egyptian Painting and Sculpture.* New York, 1992.

GREEK ART

Amyx, Darrell Arlynn. *Corinthian Vase-Painting of the Archaic Period.* Berkeley, Calif., 1988.

Beazley, John Davidson. *The Development of Attic Black-Figure.* Berkeley, Calif., 1951.

Bieber, Margarete. *The Sculpture of the Hellenistic Age.* New York, 1961.

Coldstream, John Nicholas. *Greek Geometric Pottery.* London and New York, 1968.

Getz-Preziosi, Pat. *Sculptors of the Cyclades: Individual and Tradition in the Third Millennium b.c.* Ann Arbor, Mich., 1987.

Moon, Warren G., and Louise Berge. *Greek Vase-Painting in Midwestern Collections.* Chicago, 1979.

Pedley, John Griffiths. *Greek Art and Archaeology.* London, 1992.

Pollitt, Jerome Jordan. *Art and Experience in Classical Greece.* Cambridge, 1972.

Robertson, Martin. *A Shorter History of Greek Art.* Cambridge, 1981.

_____. *The Art of Vase-Painting in Classical Athens.* Cambridge, 1992.

Smith, R. R. R. *Hellenistic Art.* London and New York, 1991.

Stewart, Andrew F. *Greek Sculpture: An Exploration.* New Haven, Conn., 1990.

Trendall, Arthur Dale. *Red Figure Vases of South Italy and Sicily.* London, 1989.

Woodford, Susan. *An Introduction to Greek Art.* Ithaca, N.Y., 1986.

ETRUSCAN ART

Andrén, Arvid. *Architectural Terracottas from Etrusco-Italic Temples.* Lund and Leipzig, 1940.

Banti, Luisa. *The Etruscan Cities and Their Culture.* Berkeley, Calif., and Los Angeles, 1973.

Bonfante, Larissa, ed. *Etruscan Life and Afterlife.* Detroit, 1986.

Brendel, Otto J. *Etruscan Art.* Harmondsworth, 1978.

De Puma, Richard. *Etruscan Tomb-Groups.* Mainz, 1986.

Haynes, Sibyl. *Etruscan Bronzes.* London, 1986.

Macnamara, Ellen. *The Etruscans.* Cambridge, Mass., 1991.

Pallottino, Massimo. *The Etruscans.* Harmondsworth, 1978.

Ridgway, David, and Francesca Serra Ridgway, eds. *Italy before the Romans.* London, 1979.

Rasmussen, Tom. *Bucchero Pottery from Southern Etruria.* Cambridge, 1979.

Sprenger, Maya, Gilda Bartoloni, and Max Hirmer. *The Etruscans.* New York, 1983.

Steingräber, Stefan. *Etruscan Painting.* New York, 1986.

ROMAN ART

Brendel, Otto J. *Prolegomena to the Study of Roman Art.* New Haven, Conn., and London, 1979.

Brilliant, Richard. *Roman Art from the Republic to Constantine.* London and New York, 1974.

Hannestad, Niels. *Roman Art and Imperial Policy.* Jutland Archaeological Society Publications, no. 9. Aarhus, 1986.

Henig, Martin, ed. *A Handbook of Roman Art: A Comprehensive Survey of All the Arts of the Roman World.* Ithaca, N.Y., 1983.

Kahler, Heinz. *Rome and Her Empire.* London, 1963.

Kleiner, Diana E. E. *Roman Sculpture.* New Haven, Conn., and London, 1992.

L'Orange, H. P. *Art Forms and Civic Life in the Late*

Roman Empire. Princeton, N.J., 1965.

Strong, Donald. *Roman Art.* 2nd ed. New York, 1988.

Toynbee, J. M. C. *The Art of the Romans.* London, 1965.

Vermeule, Cornelius C., III. *Greek Sculpture and Roman Taste: The Purpose and Setting of Graeco-Roman Art in Italy and the Greek Imperial East.* Ann Arbor, Mich., 1977.

von Heintze, Helga. *Roman Art.* New York, 1971.

Walker, Susan. *Roman Art.* London and Cambridge, Mass., 1991.

Wheeler, Mortimer. *Roman Art and Architecture.* New York, 1968.

ANCIENT GLASS

Auth, Susan H. *Ancient Glass at the Newark Museum.* Newark, N.J., 1976.

Barag, Dan P. "Glass Pilgrim Vessels from Jerusalem, Pts. I-III." *Journal of Glass Studies* 12 (1970), pp. 35–63; 13 (1971), pp. 45–63.

Goldstein, Sidney M. *Pre-Roman and Early Roman Glass in the Corning Museum of Glass.* Corning, N.Y., 1979.

Grose, David F. "The Origins and Early History of Glass." In *The History of Glass,* edited by Dan Klein and Ward Lloyd. London, 1984. Pp. 9–38.

_____. *The Toledo Museum of Art: Early Ancient Glass: Core-Formed, Rod-Formed, and Cast Vessels and Objects from the Late Bronze Age to the Early Roman Empire.* New York, 1989.

Harden, Donald B., Hansgerd Hellenkemper, Kenneth Painter, and David Whitehouse. *Glass of the Caesars,* exh. cat., The Corning Museum of Glass. Milan, 1987.

Matheson, Susan B. *Ancient Glass in the Yale University Art Gallery.* New Haven, Conn., 1980.

Nolte, Birgit. *Die Glasgefässe im alten Aegypten.* München Egyptologische Studien, no. 14. Berlin, 1968.

Oliver, Andrew, Jr. "Late Hellenistic Glass in the Metropolitan Museum." *Journal of Glass Studies* 9 (1967), pp. 13–33.

Price, Jennifer. "Glass." In *Roman Crafts,* edited by Donald Strong and David Brown. London, 1976. Pp. 111–25.

Riefstahl, Elizabeth. *Ancient Egyptian Glass and Glazes in the Brooklyn Museum,* exh. cat. Brooklyn, N.Y., 1968.

Saldern, Axel von, Birgit Nolte, Peter La Baume, and Thea Elisabeth Haevernick. *Gläser der Antike, Sammlung Erwin Oppenländer,* exh. cat., Museum für Kunst und Gewerbe. Hamburg, 1974.

Stern, E. Marianne. *The Toledo Museum of Art: Roman Mold-Blown Glass, First to Early Seventh Centuries.* Rome, forthcoming.

ANCIENT COINS

EGYPTIAN

Dattari, G. *Moneta imperiali greche: Numi Augg. Alexandrini.* Bologna, 1975.

Milne, J. G. *Catalogue of Alexandrian Coins.* Oxford, 1927; reprinted, New York, 1971.

Poole, R. S. *Catalogue of the Greek Coins in the British Museum: Alexandria.* London, 1892.

_____. *Catalogue of the Greek Coins in the British Museum: The Ptolemies, Kings of Egypt.* London, 1882.

GREEK

Carradice, I., and M. J. Price. *Coinage in the Greek World.* London, 1988.

Bellinger, A. R. *Essays on the Coinage of Alexander the Great.* New York, 1963.

Brett, A. B. *Catalogue of Greek Coins.* Museum of Fine Arts, Boston, 1955.

British Museum. *Catalogue of Greek Coins in the British Museum.* London, 1923-73.

Grose, S. W. *Catalogue of the McClean Collection of Greek Coins.* Cambridge, 1923-29.

Head, Barkley V. *Historia Numorum: A Manual of Greek Numismatics.* Oxford, 1911.

Hill, G. F. *Guide to the Principal Coins of the Greeks.* London, 1932.

Kraay, Colin M. *Archaic and Classical Greek Coins.* London, 1976.

Kraay, Colin M., and M. Hirmer. *Greek Coins.* New York, 1966.

Macdonald, G. *Catalogue of Greek Coins in the Hunterian Collection.* Glasgow, 1899-1905.

ROMAN

Crawford, M. H. *Roman Republican Coinage.* Cambridge, 1974.

Giacosa, G. *Woman of the Caesars.* Trans. R. Holloway. Milan, 1977.

Hill, P. V. *The Coinage of Septimius Severus and His Family.* London, 1977.

Kent, J. P. C., A. Hirmer, and M. Hirmer. *Roman Coins.* New York, 1978.

Mattingly, H. *Roman Coins.* London, 1977.

Roman Imperial Coinage. London, 1923-84.

Stevenson, S. W. *Dictionary of Roman Coins.* London, 1889; reprinted, London, 1964.

Sutherland, C. H. V. *Roman Coins.* London, 1974.

Sydenham, E. A. *The Coinage of the Roman Republic.* London, 1952; reprinted, New York, 1976.

Notes

ALEXANDER, "A History of the Ancient Art Collection at The Art Institute of Chicago," pp. 6–13.

1. Charles L. Hutchinson, Speech given to the Chicago Literary Club, c. 1915. Charles L. Hutchinson Papers, The Newberry Library, Chicago.

2. Old Register, Book 1, pp. 18–19, Registrar's Records, The Art Institute of Chicago Archives (hereafter referred to as AIC Archives).

3. Lenore O. Keene Congdon, ed., "The Assos Journals of Francis H. Bacon," *Archaeology* 27, 2 (Apr. 1974), p. 83.

4. William M. R. French, *Notes—Journey to Europe with Mr. and Mrs. Charles L. Hutchinson Starting from New York, Saturday, March 9, 1889*, p. 18. Office of the Director, William M. R. French, box 21, AIC Archives.

5. Ibid., p. 101. These lead pipes are no longer in the Art Institute's collection.

6. "Notes on Greek Vases in the Art Institute of Chicago," Departmental History Subject Files—Classical Department, AIC Archives.

7. Walter M. Whitehill, *The Museum of Fine Arts, Boston: A Centennial History* (Cambridge, Mass., 1970), vol. 1, p. 146.

8. French (note 4), p. 13.

9. Alfred Emerson, "The Greek Vases in the Art Institute," *Bulletin of the Art Institute of Chicago* 5, 3 (Jan. 1912), p. 43.

10. Rodolpho Lanciani to Hutchinson, Apr. 13, 1889. President of the Board of Trustees, Charles L. Hutchinson, box 1, AIC Archives; French (note 4), p. 87; Old Register (note 2), pp. 19–21.

11. French (note 4), p. 87.

12. Ibid., pp. 21–22.

13. The Art Institute of Chicago, *Catalogue of The Art Institute of Chicago: Metal Work, Graeco-Italian Vases and Antiquities* (Dec. 1889).

14. *Collection Eugene Piot—Antiquities* (Paris, 1890). This elaborately illustrated sales catalogue still casts a seductive spell. Some copies are annotated, signifying purchases made.

15. Old Register (note 2), p. 30.

16. The Art Institute of Chicago, *Catalogue of Collection of Idols belonging to W. J. Gunning*, exh. cat. (1890–91), p. 21.

17. The Art Institute of Chicago, *Catalogue of a Polychrome Exhibition*, exh. cat. (1892).

18. Ibid., p. 19.

19. Board of Trustee Records, Trustee Minutes, vol. 4, p. 95; vol. 5, p. 104; vol. 7, p. 110, AIC Archives.

20. Thomas W. Goodspeed, *Charles L. Hutchinson, 1854–1924* (Chicago, 1924), p. 50.

21. James H. Breasted to Hutchinson, Sept. 8, 1901. Hutchinson Papers (note 1).

22. Board of Trustee Records, Trustee Minutes, vol. 4, p. 243, AIC Archives.

23. Old Register (note 2), pp. 45–46.

24. Ibid., p. 46.

25. Invoice from J. Lambros, 1892, Hutchinson Papers (note 1).

26. G. C. Pier, *Historical Scarab Seals from the Art Institute* (Chicago, 1907).

27. *Bulletin of The Art Institute of Chicago* 1, 1 (Oct. 1907), pp. 12–13.

28. Q. David Bowers, "Dealers Scramble to Buy Brand Coins," *Coin World*, Nov. 23, 1983, p. 52.

29. Board of Trustee Records, Trustee Minutes, vol. 8, p. 106, AIC Archives.

30. Board of Trustee Records, Trustee Minutes, vol. 7, p. 32, AIC Archives.

31. Breasted to Hutchinson, Dec. 4, 1919. Courtesy of the Oriental Institute of the University of Chicago.

32. Board of Trustee Records, Trustee Minutes, vol. 7, p. 58, AIC Archives.

33. Breasted to Hutchinson (note 31).

34. Ibid.

35. Breasted to Hutchinson, Dec. 17, 1919. Courtesy of the Oriental Institute of the University of Chicago.

36. Theodore W. Robinson to Vester & Co., Aug. 11, 1925. Theodore W. Robinson Papers, Ancient Art Collection, The Art Institute of Chicago.

37. Azeez Khayat to Robinson, Dec. 17, 1928, Robinson Papers (note 36).

38. See list of committees in The Art Institute of Chicago, *Annual Report for the Year 1928*.

39. Richard Pratt, *David Adler* (New York, 1970), p. 197.

40. Interview with Mrs. Robert B. Mayer, June 25, 1984.

Recent Books Published by The Art Institute of Chicago

ASIAN ART IN THE ART
INSTITUTE OF CHICAGO
*Elinor Pearlstein, James T. Ulak, and
Deborah Del Gais Muller, with an
introduction by Yutaka Mino*

Published to celebrate the reopening
of the Art Institute's galleries of Asian
art, this volume presents a selection of
90 objects from the museum's Chinese, Japanese, and Korean collec-
tions. It features important examples of materials from ancient
Chinese tombs in bronze, ceramic, and jade; outstanding ceramics
from all three cultures showing the development of forms, firing,
and glazing techniques; Chinese and Japanese Buddhist sculpture;
Chinese painting; and fine examples of Japanese textiles, painted
scrolls, and screens. Also included are selections from the Art
Institute's renowned Buckingham Collection of Japanese wood-
block prints.
The Art Institute of Chicago; hardcover distributed by
Harry N. Abrams, New York
9 x 11½ in.; 152 pages; 120 color illustrations
Hardcover, $35.00, ISBN 0-8109-1916-8; softcover, $24.95,
ISBN 0-86559-095-8

ITALIAN PAINTINGS BEFORE
1600 IN THE ART INSTITUTE
OF CHICAGO: A CATALOGUE
OF THE COLLECTION
*Christopher Lloyd, with Margherita
Andreotti, Larry J. Feinberg, and
Martha Wolff*

The first in a long-awaited series of
scholarly catalogues, this volume
focuses on one of the most important
collections of early Italian paintings in
the United States. It contains comprehensive entries on close to
100 paintings, featuring an outstanding panel by the Master of the
Bigallo Crucifix, a recently rediscovered *Portrait of Alessandro de'
Medici* by Pontormo, splendid early Sienese paintings, a rare
group of Florentine *cassone* panels, and an early masterpiece by
Correggio. Each painting is accompanied by a detailed description
of its physical condition, provenance, and a critical discussion of
earlier scholarship.
The Art Institute of Chicago and Princeton University Press
8¼ x 11¼ in.; 272 pages,
175 illustrations (40 in color)
Hardcover, $90.00, ISBN 0-86559-110-5

EUROPEAN DECORATIVE
ARTS IN THE ART INSTITUTE
OF CHICAGO
*Ian Wardropper and
Lynn Springer Roberts*

This stunning publication introduces
readers to the legacy of European
artisans, ranging from the anonymous
craftsmen of the early Middle Ages to
the celebrated designers of the Bau-
haus in the 1920s. Focusing on 62 outstanding objects from the
Art Institute's holdings of European decorative arts, this book
conveys the unique beauty of each work in fine full-color reproductions, while evoking a sense of the time, place, and taste that
gave birth to it. The selection represents the wealth of mediums
and types—ceramics, furniture, glass, ivory, and silver, to name a
few.
The Art Institute of Chicago; hardcover distributed by
Harry N. Abrams, New York
9 x 11½ in.; 140 pages; 94 color illustrations
Hardcover, $35.00, ISBN 0-8109-3253-9; softcover, $24.95,
ISBN 0-86559-090-7

CHICAGO ARCHITECTURE
AND DESIGN, 1923-1993:
RECONFIGURATION OF AN
AMERICAN METROPOLIS
Edited by John Zukowsky

The companion volume to the
museum's award-winning book
Chicago Architecture, 1872-1922, this
major new study places Chicago's
20th-century architecture in a broad,
sociocultural context. Seventeen essays address a wide array of
topics: electrification and lighting; the history of airports; the creation of new business centers on the city's periphery; shopping in
Chicago and suburbia; the development of the postwar skyscraper;
public housing; air-rights projects; and modern postwar houses.
The book contains a large section of color and duotone plates, an
architectural genealogy, and a biographical glossary of important
architects, developers, planners, and others.
The Art Institute of Chicago and Prestel Verlag, Munich
9 x 12 in.; 460 pages, 630 illustrations (80 in color)
Hardcover, $75.00, ISBN 3-7913-1251-0; softcover, $39.95,
ISBN 0-86559-109-1

*All of these books are available from The Art Institute of Chicago
Museum Shop, as well as from three additional Museum Shop locations: 900 North Michigan Avenue, fifth floor; Oakbrook Center;
and the Woodfield Mall. Art Institute members receive a 10% discount on all purchases at each location. For more information concerning the Museum Shops, call (312) 443-3536.*

Recent and Forthcoming Issues of *Museum Studies*

MUSEUM STUDIES, Vol. 18, No. 1
*Five Centuries of Japanese Kimono:
On This Sleeve of Fondest Dreams*

This issue was prepared in conjunction with a celebrated exhibition of the Art Institute's traditional Japanese costumes. The essays in this issue delve into the cultural and art-historical background of these lavish costumes, most of which were intended for use in Noh theater. This issue also includes an introductory discussion of Noh theater, an essay on a series of prints by the Japanese master Utamaro depicting the process of silk-making, and a portfolio highlighting the Art Institute's collection of kimono pattern books. A spectacular color-plate section reproduces the costumes displayed in the Art Institute's exhibition.
Spring 1992; 104 pages; 91 illustrations (27 in color); $14.95

MUSEUM STUDIES, Vol. 18, No. 2
*British Art: Recent Acquisitions and
Discoveries at the Art Institute*

This issue focuses on the growing collection of British art at the Art Institute. A foreword by Art Institute curator Martha Tedeschi discusses the place of British art in the museum's permanent collection. The essays that follow examine a previously unknown portrait study by James McNeill Whistler, a dramatic biblical painting by Philippe Jacques de Loutherbourg, a marvelous self-portrait by Joseph Wright of Derby, a masterpiece in silver by Omar Ramsden and Alwyn Carr, and two works by members of the Pre-Raphaelite circle––Dante Gabriel Rossetti and Simeon Solomon.
Fall 1992; 88 pages; 66 illustrations; $10.50

MUSEUM STUDIES, Vol. 19, No. 1
*One Hundred Years at the Art
Institute: A Centennial Celebration*

This issue, devoted entirely to the history of the Art Institute, commemorates the 100th anniversary of the museum's renowned Michigan Avenue building. Essays discuss the revolutionary 1913 Armory Show and its tumultuous effect on Chicago; the trailblazing career of Daniel Catton Rich, distinguished director of the Art Institute from 1938 to 1958; and the ground-breaking exhibition of the Arensberg Collection of modern art at the museum in 1949. This issue also features a lavish duotone section of archival photographs documenting the history of the Art Institute from 1893 to 1933.
Spring 1993; 112 pages; 105 illustrations (40 in duotone); $14.95

MUSEUM STUDIES, Vol. 19, No. 2
*Notable Acquisitions at The Art
Institute of Chicago since 1980*

The objects discussed in this issue were selected by James N. Wood, Director and President of the Art Institute, and are representative of the many important acquisitions made by the museum since 1980. Essays examine a diverse and fascinating group of works: Constantin Brancusi's masterpiece *Golden Bird*; five Japanese works including prints by Katsushika Hokusai and a portrait of Daruma, the first patriarch of Zen Buddhism; a remarkable West African drum by a Senufo master sculptor; a superb late nineteenth-century upright piano by the British designer Mackay Hugh Baillie Scott; and an intriguing still life by the American photographer Paul Strand. A color-plate section features the principal works in the issue.
Fall 1993; 96 pages; 71 illustrations (8 in color); $10.50

MUSEUM STUDIES, Vol. 20, No. 2
*A Living Tradition: The Joseph
Winterbotham Collection at The Art
Institute of Chicago*

Joseph Winterbotham left a remarkable legacy to the Art Institute. His gift of $50,000 to the museum in 1921 stipulated that the Art Institute should assemble a collection of 35 European paintings. The unique terms of this gift have resulted in one of the most distinguished collections of 19th- and 20th-century paintings in the world. In this special issue of *Museum Studies*, an introductory essay on the Winterbotham family is followed by entries on the works in the collection. All of the featured works are reproduced in color.
Fall 1994; 96 pages; 95 illustrations (35 in color); $14.95

All issues of Museum Studies *are available from The Art Institute of Chicago Museum Shop, as well as from three additional Museum Shop locations: 900 North Michigan Avenue, fifth floor; Oakbrook Center; and Woodfield Mall. Art Institute members receive a 10% discount on all purchases at each location. For more information concerning the Museum Shops, call (312) 443-3536. Museum Studies is also available by mail from the Publications Department, The Art Institute of Chicago, 111 South Michigan Avenue, Chicago, Illinois 60603-6110 (please make checks payable to* Museum Studies*). Subscription information can be found on the inside front cover of this issue.*